# BERLITZ®

CW00602002

# TORONTO

**1991/1992 Edition**

**By the staff of Berlitz Guides**

Copyright © 1991, 1986 by Berlitz Publishing S.A.,
Avenue d'Ouchy 61, 1000 Lausanne 6, Switzerland.

Berlitz Trademark Reg. U.S. Patent Office and other countries.
Library of Congress Catalog Card No. 85-81794.

Printed in Switzerland by Weber S.A., Bienne.

**4th Printing**
**1991/1992 Edition**

**Updated or revised 1991, 1989**

# How to use our guide

- All the **practical information,** hints and tips that you will need before or during your trip start on page 106.

- For **general background,** see the sections The City and the People, page 6, and A Brief History, page 12.

- All the **sights** to see in Toronto are listed between pages 24 and 53. Sights and pleasures within striking distance of Toronto are described between pages 53 and 84. Our own choice of sights most highly recommended is pinpointed by the Berlitz traveller symbol.

- **Sports, entertainment** and all other **leisure activities** are analyzed between pages 85 and 97, while information on **restaurants and cuisine** is to be found on pages 98 to 104.

- Finally, there is an **index** at the back of the book, pages 126 to 128.

---

*Found an error or an omission in this Berlitz Guide? Or a change or new feature we should know about? Our editor would be happy to hear from you, and a postcard would do. Be sure to include your name and address, since in appreciation for a useful suggestion, we'd like to send you a free travel guide. Write to: Berlitz Publishing S.A., Avenue d'Ouchy 61, 1000 Lausanne 6, Switzerland.*

    *Although we make every effort to ensure the accuracy of all the information in this book, changes occur incessantly. We cannot therefore take responsibility for facts, prices, addresses and circumstances in general that are constantly subject to alteration.*

---

Text: Suzanne Patterson
Staff Editor: Christina Jackson
Photography: Erling Mandelmann
Layout: Doris Haldemann
We wish to express our thanks to Nick Campbell, Rick Morris and Martha Campbell for their help in the preparation of this guide. We are also grateful to Air Canada and the offices of the Ontario Ministry of Tourism in Toronto, Ottawa and Paris, with special thanks to Isabelle Galy-Ashé for invaluable assistance.
Cartography: Falk-Verlag, Hamburg.

# Contents

## Maps

*Downtown Toronto p.37, Metropolitan Toronto p.45, Niagara Falls p.54, Lower Ontario pp.60–61, Ottawa p.80.*

*Cover photo:* Toronto skyline; *photo pp.2–3:* Fun and games at Ontario Place **5**

# The City and the People

Toronto's rise to stardom among cities is no secret. It's also nothing short of a modern miracle. Once a provincial backwater and the butt of derisory jokes, Toronto has metamorphosed into a dynamic, vibrant metropolis of over 2 million, the financial and industrial heart of Canada.

Visually it offers a taut contrast between glossy, contemporary buildings and older churches and houses that have been staunchly protected by conservation-minded citizens. The city's situation itself is glorious: bounded by the Don and Humber river valleys and set on a series of ravines by the expanse of Lake Ontario, it overlooks the harbor and a scattering of verdant islands.

While many people call the suburbs home, many more live

in the heart of town in renovated houses or modern apartment blocks. Toronto's "neighborhoods" are populated by a rollicking ethnic cast. Toronto reputedly has more Italian inhabitants than Florence. The Chinese, Hungarians and West Indians all have their own communities,

*Functional and fun—Toronto's high-rise reflections and a bicycle-car made for two.*

too. One blends into another— offering color and humor and exotic sights, sounds and fragrances in lively profusion.

It wasn't always so. Long a humble trading post, settled by French traders in the 17th century, Toronto served briefly as capital of Upper Canada, thanks to Lieutenant-Governor John Graves Simcoe, who founded the city in 1793 and called it York, after George III's son, Frederick, Duke of York. But poor "Muddy York"

*Tartan tradition brings echoes of past to super-modern present.*

never got very far as capital —especially after Americans burned down most of the settlement during the War of 1812.

York's fortunes revived as refugees from Europe settled here in the wake of the Napoleonic Wars. Finally, with incorporation in 1834, the town took back its original Indian name, Toronto, which means "meeting place". Power was in the hands of a group of Anglo-Saxon lawyers, bankers and financiers known as the Family Compact, who also laid down

life went on in the same staid way. But then, shortly after World War II, a huge influx of immigrants from the four corners of the earth started to change the face and soul of the city. The St. Lawrence Seaway opened, linking Toronto to the trading nations of the world. Manufacturing industries along Lake Ontario boomed, and business flourished in the 1970s as many head offices from Montreal relocated in Toronto.

The 1984 opening of Toronto's multimillion-dollar Convention Centre merely set the seal on a well-known fact: Toronto held the heartbeat of the country's business—and just about everything else as well. The strict "blue laws" regulating drinking and commerce on Sundays which drove everybody off the streets— sometimes all the way to Buffalo—were repealed, and weekends in Toronto became fun.

Now it's Americans who cross the border, headed for Toronto, with its cosmopolitan atmosphere and lively entertainment. The Old Guard may be pursing their lips in private, but everyone admits the new-look Toronto is exciting—and good for business, as well.

rigid moral laws for Toronto. Immersed in stuffy puritanical traditions, the city earned itself the epithet "Toronto the Good".

When Ottawa was designated capital of the united Province of Canada in 1855, Toronto seemed hardly to notice, and for almost a century

Toronto is the hub of Ontario—a vast province of 1,068,582 square kilometers

(417,000 sq. mi.), greater in area than France and Spain together. Agriculture and mining flourish, along with banking and industry, which includes everything from manufacturing cars to producing microchips. But the population density is so low that you don't have to go far to find wide, open spaces and forested lakeland—even uncharted wilderness.

In eastern Ontario, the nation's capital, Ottawa, has undergone a rejuvenation of its own and offers a wealth of natural and man-made beauties.

Many visitors to Ontario may go no further than Niagara Falls; others plan their leisure days around the marvelous Shakespeare festival in Stratford or the Shaw Festival in Niagara-on-the-Lake, both of which are summer events.

But Toronto attracts year-round, with everything a big city can offer. Activity goes on night and day. Joggers get out early, while in the evenings there are classical and rock concerts, ballet, theater and movies. Cabaret acts and discos round out the night scene, and there are endless fairs and festivals.

Getting around is easy—by the slick subway (underground), taxi or frequent buses, if you don't have your own car.

And walking is a real pleasure, since it's both scenic and safe to walk most streets at all hours.

Eating out can be anything, from fast food or vegetarian cooking to the haughtiest of French *haute cuisine*. You can spend an evening in a raucous spaghetti parlor or German beer-hall, or in any number of ethnic restaurants.

Toronto is something of a shopper's paradise. From fashionable Bloor Street to the magnificent high-tech Eaton Centre to the harbor, thousands of shops lure you in with tempting displays and bargains. Antique-collectors browse in the big Harbourfront markets,

while other shoppers check out the countless attractive boutiques. Many of the city's shops seem to be underground in one of the new subsurface malls, a practical alternative when winter winds blow and a cool respite when summer days get too warm.

The weather extremes don't faze Ontarians, who take advantage of every season. Spring and fall offer typical North American pleasures—a pastel palette of flowers and blossoming trees in the spring, a riot of primary colors as fall changes maples and birch to flaming red or yellow against the green conifers.

If summer heat and humidity occasionally edge up to wilting levels, there is plenty of green parkland to resort to, plus Lake Ontario and some 400,000 smaller lakes to cool off in. Winter brings sub-zero temperatures, but the frozen landscape is appealing and people take to their ice skates and cross-country skis.

Toronto also offers incomparable museums, including the Royal Ontario Museum, with its large collection of Buddhist art and paleonto-

*In Toronto, you're a subway ride from almost anywhere.*

logy, and the new Gardiner Museum, specializing in rare porcelains. Ontario Place is a delightful setting for an outdoor summer theater, cinema, Canadian exhibits and other less serious amusements. In the Don Valley, the spectacular Ontario Science Centre has so much to see and do that adults are more reluctant to go home than children. In another valley further east, the Metro Zoo houses animals from Canada and all over the world.

You can meet people easily —in cafés, boutiques, museums. Everyone seems relaxed, ready to talk. Canada is officially bilingual—English and French—but English is the preferred language in Toronto, although some Torontonians still converse in Latvian, Cantonese Chinese or some other exotic tongue.

Your accent doesn't matter here. Because in Toronto and all over Ontario, "body language" is universal and people know how to smile broadly. They have no formal rules of etiquette—how could they, coming from such diverse places as Athens and Barbados? There may still be problems, but somehow, in this melting pot of languages, races and creeds, the harmony seems complete.

# A Brief History

The first human beings to come to the North American continent some 50,000 years ago were nomadic peoples who crossed from northeast Asia via the Bering Strait in the wake of the last Ice Age. Over several millennia they spread southward through Mexico, dividing into clans and tribes with their own languages and cultures.

In what is now Canada, the tribes evolved in various ways. Some lived off the bounty of the sea, others were farmers, hunters and foragers. But all these native or Indian and Inuit (Eskimo) tribes were still living in primitive, stone-age conditions, ignorant of the wheel and iron, when European explorers arrived in the 16th century.

### New France
After the discoveries of Columbus, the ambitious French King Francis I (1515–47) commissioned Giovanni da Verrazzano in 1524 to sail across the ocean and stake France's claim in the New World. Ten years later, Jacques Cartier, looking for a northwest passage to Asia, came to the Gulf of St. Lawrence. He sailed up the river to a place called Hoche-

laga, which he named Mont Réal (Mount Royal) for the majestic-looking hill which dominated the village. In the name of France, Cartier called the lands Kannata, the Algonquin word for "settlement".

After that, French enthusiasm waned for about 75 years, until a fad for beaver hats and trim under the reign of Francis II opened up new possibilities for the fur trade. But it wasn't only furs that attracted the French to Canada; they also recognized the vast, untapped mineral and timber resources, as well as its strategic value as a base in case of war with Spain. And missionaries sought to spread Christianity among the new-found heathens.

Thus, in 1603-4 Samuel de Champlain sailed up the St. Lawrence and Ottawa rivers to the place where Ottawa now stands. Much of the land was claimed as New France, and in 1608 Champlain founded Quebec, which later became the first main town-settlement.

At this time, the Toronto area was inhabited by Indians. Samuel de Champlain sent his young companion Etienne Brûlé there in 1615 to establish friendly relations, which he did —living with the Indians and learning their language. It wasn't until 1750 that the site was considered important enough for a fort—little more than a storage house at that. But, as the fur trade picked up, a stronger fort, Rouillé, was built by the French to intercept Indians trading with the British across the lake.

Throughout the 17th century, the French made deep inroads into the American interior, as far as the Rocky Mountains and south to the Gulf of Mexico. They founded Detroit, St. Louis and New Orleans, and claimed most of the Midwest. Louis Jolliet and Father Marquette were the first Europeans to see the Mississippi River.

The British were also in the colonizing business, establishing settlements along most of the American Eastern Seaboard from Maine down to Georgia. In 1610, Henry Hudson, in the service of the Dutch East India Company, discovered the enormous bay that bears his name, and in 1670 the Hudson's Bay Company—even today an important Canadian retailing organization—was founded by the British to promote the fur trade.

The Indians themselves had not gained much from the coming of the white man. Diseases from Europe, to which they **13** had no immunity, ravaged the population. They were seduced by whisky and other alcoholic concoctions. And the introduction of guns and metal weapons gave fresh and deadly impetus to the feuds between the southern Iroquois tribes and the Hurons to the north. From the 1640s to the '60s, they clashed violently, terrorizing and killing any Europeans who happened to be in the way.

The French and the British had their own battles to fight. Rivalry between the two European powers had been carried over to the New World, and the stage was being set for confrontation. In Canada, the Indians were undecided in their loyalties, but mostly they sided with the French. After vicious fighting, the British marched on Fort Frontenac in 1758, outmaneuvering the French for an easy victory. The British went on to take the fort at Niagara the following year. When the news reached the French, they burned down Fort Rouillé to keep it out of British hands.

After a protracted battle for Quebec City, on the night of September 12, 1759, General James Wolfe managed to sneak 4,500 British soldiers behind the city's defenses, surprising the French and their astute and capable leader, Louis, Marquis de Montcalm. The ensuing battle on the Plains of Abraham was brief and bloody. Both leaders perished in the fray: Wolfe survived just long enough to hear of his victory; Montcalm died of his wounds a few hours later. After a five-day siege, Quebec surrendered.

Here the fate of the North American continent was more or less decided. Following the Treaty of Paris in 1763, the British took over administration of the territory. New France was nothing more than an idle dream, although a French presence and influence in Canada would always remain.

## Americans and Loyalists

By 1775 the restive, rebellious American colonies south of Canada were seething with discontent, and the resultant revolution was to make its mark on Canada as well. Among the colonists' grievances was the Quebec Act of 1774, by which the British Parliament intended to provide French Canadians with a more suitable and fairer form of government. But the Protestants in America saw this as a dangerous concession to Roman Catholicism. They decided to eliminate the French threat by marching on Canada.

In November 1775, the Continental Army set out

under generals Richard Montgomery and Benedict Arnold —who was later convicted of treason. Montgomery's forces took Montreal, but the general was killed. Arnold's troops faced a British-French alliance in Quebec and failed to capture the city. In 1776, more pressing matters—the American Revolution—caused the Americans to abandon their bid to take control of Canada.

During and after the revolution, the Loyalists, American colonists who had remained loyal to the British crown, were obliged to flee to safer territory in Canada, some 7,000 of them to Ontario. Canada also attracted other ambitious Americans from south of the border, opportunists who wanted to take advantage of the grants of free land offered to Loyalists.

The Canada Act of 1791 split

*Hard work and hope of early settlers built today's Canada.*

the colony into two provinces, Lower Canada (Quebec)—mainly populated by the original settlers or *Canadiens*—and Upper Canada (Ontario), stronghold of the Loyalists, with its capital at Niagara-on-the-Lake. Each was headed by a lieutenant-governor.

In 1792 the Lieutenant-Governor of Upper Canada, John Graves Simcoe, moved the capital from Niagara-on-the-Lake to London for strategic reasons—the former was too close to the American border. But London was also vulnerable, and finally, in 1793, Toronto was chosen as capital and renamed York.

The new capital was swampy, unattractive and unpromising in every way. Undaunted, Simcoe encouraged construction and development, including the building of Yonge Street, which would cut right up through the province to Lake Simcoe, to the north of the city.

The Canadians were not left long in peace by their American neighbors. British attempts to disrupt America's Atlantic trade routes led to the War of 1812, and the Americans invaded Canada while the British were busy fighting Napoleon's forces in Europe. But the Americans were relying on support from the Canadian Indians—who finally decided, with a few exceptions, to side with the British.

Still underpopulated, Upper Canada was defended by only 1,600 British soldiers led by Major-General Isaac Brock, who won some early victories, notably at Fort Michilimackinac, where Lake Huron meets Lake Michigan. The American forces attacking Montreal were demoralized and gave up without a battle. A big American thrust on the Niagara Frontier in October 1812 was finally repulsed by the British with their Indian allies, but the death of Brock during the battle was a blow to the British. Another notable leader, the Shawnee chief Tecumseh died during the Battle of the Thames River.

In April 1813, as the war dragged on, the Americans burned and looted York and Niagara-on-the-Lake. The British retaliated with an attack on Washington in 1814 that gave the White House its final look and name: blackened by smoke, it had to be repainted white and has been that way ever since.

The war finally ran out of steam and was officially ended with the Treaty of Ghent in 1814, though skirmishes continued along the borders for years.

## The Loyalists

They came from every class and walk of life. Lawyers and laborers, clergymen, soldiers and farmers, craftsmen, scholars and peasants, Iroquois Indians, immigrants and black African slaves.

Their motives ranged from the noblest to the most self-seeking. But, political or personal, the one common aim that united this extraordinary mixture of people was the defense of the United Empire.

It wasn't easy in the 13 rebel colonies for the 250,000 stalwarts who remained loyal to the Crown. Regarded as traitors, they were harassed, occasionally beaten up or tarred and feathered, and often driven out of their communities. Loyalists lost their voting rights, were unable to sell land or recover debts and suddenly found it impossible to become lawyers, doctors and teachers.

Then, after almost ten years of hostility and humiliation, came the bitter pill: the Treaty of Paris (1783), which acknowledged the independence of the United States. For the Loyalists who had stayed, it meant only one thing—immediate exile.

Of more than 80,000 Loyalists who fled during the period, half went to England and the British West Indies. In 1783 alone, almost 30,000 went by sea to Nova Scotia, tripling its population. Thousands of others trekked by ox cart and on foot to the St. Lawrence River and the shores of Lake Ontario.

They were far from pioneers, and ill equipped to deal with the rigors of their new life in Canada. Many died.

Six years later, Britain acknowledged the Loyalists' contribution by announcing that all those who had remained loyal were entitled to add the letters U.E. (United Empire) to their names. The privilege was extended to their families and descendants—a distinction that proved useful in terms of social and financial standing.

You'll still find the initials appearing in parts of Ontario today.

## Growth and Consolidation

York and the rest of Canada expanded as refugees fled the Napoleonic Wars and the sweatshop conditions of the Industrial Revolution in Great Britain. In 1834 York was incorporated and took back its original Indian name, Toronto.

At this time, factions in both Upper and Lower Canada were moving toward revolt. In Lower Canada, French-speaking Canadians were agitating 17 for government more responsible to the people. Fighting broke out in November 1837 and the rebels fought several pitched battles with British troops before finally being defeated in 1838.

In Upper Canada another rebellion was brewing—this one directed against the privileged group known as the Family Compact, who held the reins of power. The instigator of the revolt was William Lyon Mackenzie, a fearless Scot, editor of *The Colonial Advocate* and supporter of a more broadly democratic government than that offered by the conservative ruling elite. In December 1837, Mackenzie and his followers attempted to enter Toronto to overthrow the government, but were quickly overcome; Mackenzie fled to the United States, where he remained in exile.

The British parliament took note of the discontent, appointing as governor-general Lord Durham, who recommended "anglification" as a neat solution for both Upper and Lower Canada. In 1841, Great Britain created the united Province of Canada—comprising both main provinces—as a concession to the people's desire for more independence, and William Lyon Mackenzie was allowed to return home.

As Canada's vast resources were realized—especially Ontario's lumber industry—new waves of immigrants poured into the region. Canals were built to transport goods and further unite the country; these included the Welland linking Fort Erie to Niagara-on-the-Lake, and the Rideau joining Kingston to Ottawa.

As Canada prospered, Toronto remained the center of a wealthy Protestant elite, whose strait-laced principles kept the city under a tight rein well into the 20th century.

**Independence**
Meanwhile, a rift was growing between Protestant English Canada and Catholic French Canada. Soon it became clear to everyone—French-Canadian and British-Canadian and British alike—that Canada would have to have its own democratic form of government. After long negotiations, the Dominion of Canada was created on July 1, 1867, with the passing of the British North America Act. Upper Canada, or Canada West, became Ontario (from the Indian name for "beautiful lake") and Lower

18

*Matching colors for yesterday's Indian chief in today's setting.*

Canada, or Canada East, became Quebec.

Queen Victoria had already chosen Ottawa as a suitable capital for the united Province of Canada in 1855, partly because she'd seen an attractive watercolor of the site and partly because she thought it would be a more neutral location than British-oriented Toronto or French-oriented Montreal.

The first prime minister was Sir John A. Macdonald, an influential architect of Canada's constitution, who envisaged a great nation stretching from ocean to ocean. The four founding provinces included Quebec, Ontario, New Brunswick and Nova Scotia. But provision was made for others and, shortly after the turn of the century, Canada indeed reached from coast to coast.

However, power was not concentrated exclusively in a central federal government, thanks mainly to one Oliver Mowat. Born of Scottish parents in Kingston, Ontario, Mowat was elected Premier of Ontario in 1872 and for the next 24 years fought many verbal battles to win sovereign rights for the provincial parliaments. As a result, the provinces achieved a good deal of autonomy—a principle which is still working today.

## Modern Times

Toward the end of the 19th century, Canada, already profiting from lumber and agriculture, started to exploit its formidable mineral potential. Oil was struck around the southern tip of Lake Huron; copper and nickel were discovered at Copper Cliff and Sudbury in 1883; and subsequently silver and gold were found. Much later —in 1948—the discovery of uranium precipitated a brand new mining boom.

Meanwhile, travel and commerce had been enhanced by the completion in 1885 of the Canadian Pacific Railway linking the east and west coasts— a stunning feat of engineering and sheer human will-power and drive.

Toronto was usually well apart from the French-English strife that so often convulsed Quebec. A concession to the French-speaking Canadians came in 1896, when Sir Wilfrid Laurier, a French Roman Catholic, was elected prime minister. He stayed in office until 1911 and, as a moderate, staunchly resisted any involvement of the church in state matters.

In World War I, Canada fought alongside Great Britain, although many French-Canadians objected to conscription.

## Famous Ontarians

Ontario is proud not only of the early "movers and shakers" of industry, but of some of the great intellectual, artistic and scientific achievements of its people.

Among the scientists, Frederick G. Banting and Charles H. Best discovered insulin, Dr. Murray Barr contributed important work on the determination of sex by cell analysis and James Collip isolated the hormone ACTH.

Alexander Graham Bell, inventor of the telephone, moved with his family to Brantford from Scotland as a young man, and carried out many of his experiments in Canada.

The famous Group of Seven artists forged ahead with their own, dynamic ways of seeing and painting the Canadian wilderness.

Distinguished writers from Ontario include Margaret Atwood, Morley Callaghan and Robertson Davies. In the musical world, the late Glenn Gould is still recognized as one of Bach's greatest interpreters. Maureen Forrester, chairman of the Canada Council, is a renowned mezzo-soprano. And Torontonian Oscar Peterson is still exciting audiences all over the world with his well-tempered jazz piano.

The film stars to hail from Toronto are Mary Pickford (whose house is a landmark on University Avenue), and Raymond Massey and Jason Robards Jr., both of whom came from distinguished Toronto families.

Following the war, further waves of immigrants arrived from all over central and eastern Europe.

In World War II, Canada stood firmly with the Allies, losing more than 40,000 men. Prime minister throughout the war effort was William Lyon Mackenzie King (a descendant of that famous fiery Scot).

An explosion of immigration and economic development followed the war, as the vast mineral potential was further tapped and industry drew on a large pool of new talent. The stolid city of Toronto was gradually transformed by skilled and energetic newcomers from Greece, Poland, China, Pakistan, Italy and the West Indies.

In 1959, Queen Elizabeth II and President Dwight D. Eisenhower jointly opened the St. Lawrence Seaway—a vast engineering *tour de force* that brought Canada and the United States into closer coopera-

*Fiesta time illustrates Toronto's historically happy ethnic mix.*

tion and made it possible for Toronto to become a major port.

Banking and industrial interests turned away somewhat from troubled Montreal to Toronto, creating a new boom in the 1970s. Toronto remained on the whole untouched by the British-French rivalries and separatism that had caused major national problems. It just hummed along. Shining skyscrapers shot up around Bay Street—the Wall Street of Canada—alongside some quaint Victorian buildings and a rejuvenated waterfront. Some excellent urban planners, kept on their toes by the constant battle between progressives and conservationists, have contrived to keep an attractive mix of historical atmosphere along with the latest contemporary buildings.

Today business is still thriving and the ethnic mix, far from causing social tensions, adds a colorful and lively element to what has become one of the most interesting and exciting cities in Canada.

# Facts and Figures

**Geography:** Ontario is Canada's largest province after Quebec, with an area of 1,068,582 sq. km. (417,000 sq. mi.). Bordered by Quebec to the east and by Manitoba to the west, Ontario has approximately 400,000 freshwater lakes and 1,094 km. (680 mi.) of coastline along the James and Hudson bays in the north, plus 3,710 km. (2,300 mi.) along the Great Lakes and St. Lawrence Seaway.

Toronto stands on an almost land-locked harbor on the northwest shore of Lake Ontario. Its larger urban area (Metro Toronto) is 620 sq. km. (240 sq. mi.).

Ottawa lies 490 km. (295 mi.) northeast of Toronto at the confluence of the Ottawa, Rideau and Gatineau rivers.

**Population:** Toronto: 612,000 (urban), 3,427,000 (metropolitan); Ottawa: 301,000 (urban), 819,000 (metropolitan).

**Government:** Canada is a constitutional monarchy with a parliamentary system of government. Canada forms part of the British Commonwealth; the official head of state is Britain's Queen Elizabeth II, represented by a governor-general—chosen by elected representatives of the Canadian people. Head of government is the prime minister, leader of the party holding the most seats in Parliament. Parliament consists of the House of Commons, its members elected by direct suffrage, and the Senate, its members appointed by the party in power in the House.

Canada is a federal country consisting of ten provinces and two northern territories. The capital is Ottawa. All provinces elect their own legislature to govern regional matters.

Toronto is governed by a Metro Council (whose chairman is appointed by the province of Ontario), a city council and five suburban councils.

**Religion:** Protestants of various denominations hold a slight majority in Ontario, but there are also a great number of Roman Catholics. Most other creeds—Muslim, Buddhist, Greek Orthodox, etc.—are represented.

# What to See

Toronto is organized on a sensible grid pattern, so it is quite easy to get around, whether by the efficient public transport, taxi or private car. Look at a map and note the main south-north arteries: Spadina and University avenues, Bay Street ("Banking Street"), commercial Yonge Street and Church Street. Yonge Street constitutes more or less the backbone of the city. It was constructed in 1795 as a military road leading 1,883 kilometers (1,170 mi.) north to Lake Simcoe, and now the entire street system is hinged on it. The main east-west intersections (going northward from Lake Ontario) are: Front, King, Queen, Dundas, College-Carlton and Bloor streets. All street names on the north-south axis are indicated by blue signs, east-west streets by yellow signs.

In this guide we start the sightseeing downtown near the waterfront, and make our way northward, with detours east and west. But you can easily choose your own tour of Toronto to fit your schedule and interests.

*Back to the future—adults and children pause to take in the space-age aspect of Ontario Place.*

# Waterfront Area

A great way to get oriented is a trip up the **CN Tower**, which pierces Toronto's sky like a gigantic hypodermic needle. At 553.3 meters (l,815 ft. 5 in.), it beats Chicago's Sears Tower and several other giants for the title of the world's highest free-standing structure. Built between 1973 and 1975, by Canadian National (CN), the government railroad and telecommunications firm, the tower is not only a radio and television transmission mast, but also a sure-fire tourist attraction.

If your stomach drops away as the outdoor plexiglass elevator rushes upward, consider that the speed of ascent is 6 metres (20 ft.) per second. First stop—more than 300 meters (1,122 ft.) up—is the **Sky Pod**, which has several decks from which to admire the view. Up here, too, is the world's highest restaurant and nightclub. From this level you can look out over the whole of Toronto, with its many ravines, parks and neighborhoods. To the south, you'll see the lively waterfront and harbor, dotted with sails in summer, and out to the islands. That futuristic leisure complex to the west is Ontario Place. Many of the gleaming buildings of the financial core, just **25** northeast of the CN Tower, were designed by famous architects such as Mies van der Rohe and I. M. Pei.

Another elevator takes you up to the **Space Deck**, which at 447 meters (1,465 ft.) affords distant views—they say all the way to Niagara Falls and Buffalo, U.S.A., on a clear day.

From this dizzying height you can also catch a glimpse of the newest addition to Toronto's skyline, the capacious **Metro Toronto Convention Centre**, opened in 1984. It boasts the latest in convention facilities, with three main halls to host receptions of up to 12,000 people. Banquet halls, other reception rooms and a Grand Ball Room offer more space. And of course, all are provided with the latest audiovisual equipment. Adjoining the Centre is l'Hôtel, with every possible modern amenity in sporting equipment and fast communications.

**Harbourfront**, at one time a swampy, rundown area, has been spruced up in recent years to serve as a recreation and cultural complex. New highrises have been built and the old warehouses dramatically renovated to house shops, cafés, a theater and exhibition center. The Harbourfront Antique Market at 222 Queen's Quay

(pronounced "key" in Toronto) West offers a lively assortment of bargains from ancient china to modern crafts.

The old **Redpath Sugar Factory**, at 95 Queen's Quay East, has been turned into a museum. You can see the machinery and equipment used for sugar production, as well as a film on the harvesting and processing of sugar.

The **Toronto Islands**, facing Harbourfront, are a favorite summer respite and picnic place for Torontonians. Once a peninsula and part of the Scarborough Bluffs just east of the city center, these picturesque islands were broken off by a raging storm in 1858. Today they are joined by bridges so that you can walk or cycle the length of them.

Ferry boats (no cars; you may rent bicycles on the islands) leave regularly in the summer from the docks behind the Toronto Hilton Harbour Castle at the foot of Bay Street, calling at the three main islands. **Centre Island** is the most popular, but its beach and picnic areas can be crowded. **Ward's Island** is favored by some for its lively boardwalk. (Between Centre and Ward's islands is the exclusive Royal Canadian Yacht Club, worth a visit if you belong to an affi-

*Happiness is... a hula-hoop in the park and unlimited time to play.*

liated organization or have a friend who will take you there.) **Hanlan's Point**, alongside Toronto Island Airport, has a beach along the western side.

Another way to enjoy the harbor scene is to take a three-hour launch tour, one of several boat tours offered. These also provide excellent views of downtown Toronto.

West along the waterfront, you reach **Ontario Place**, a major attraction for visitors and Torontonians alike. Built on three man-made islands, this charming 39-hectare (96-acre) park is part Disneyland, part cultural center, cleverly blended into a green waterside setting. Below a grassy knoll, the Forum amphitheater seats up to 11,000 people for its superb outdoor classical, jazz and pop concerts.

You can't miss the Cinesphere, the white geodesic dome that reminds most people of a half-buried golf ball. Inside, on a curved screen six stories high, are shown films on almost every subject, ranging from volcanic eruptions to earth and space exploration; films change every year.

Mounted on stilts, the Pod Complex offers a banqueting room, a video show and the Yours to Discover Theater.

The Children's Village is beautifully and imaginatively designed for youngsters aged from 4 to 14. There's a waterslide down a miniature mountain; a series of duck ponds for toddlers to splash in; an outsize trampoline; a children's theater and myriad other delights. And before you move on, you can put your drenched kids through the huge "dryer" shaped like a bird.

All age groups are fascinated by a tour of the destroyer **HMCS Haida**, moored at the entrance to the park; named after the Haida Indians of British Columbia, the Canadian warship saw action in World War II and the Korean War. Any nautical questions will be readily answered by Canadian sea cadets, who will also do their best to stop the younger visitors starting another war.

Just inland from Ontario

Place, **Exhibition Place** stages the annual Canadian National Exhibition, along with other events during the year, such as the Canadian International Air Show, an aquatic show and the Scottish World Festival Tattoo.

Toronto's maritime history is graphically illustrated in the **Marine Museum of Upper Canada** (Exhibition Place, just west of Princes' Gate). It's located in what used to be the officers' quarters of Stanley Barracks, a military fortification dating back to 1841. Displays show the economic and cultural changes brought about in certain areas by ships, as trading expanded along the St. Lawrence Basin and the waterways of central Canada.

Among the oddities are hooters, diving helmets, relics from sunken river vessels and the bridge of a famous old lake steamer. If you're intrigued by the museum's scale-model ships, you'll also be fascinated by a tour of the *Ned Hanlan,* a full-size tugboat in dry dock outside that was named after a famous oarsman.

Five minutes away by foot, at the center of Exhibition Park (just off Lakeshore Boulevard West), is **Canada's Sports Hall of Fame**, a national sports museum showing thousands of sporting aspirations and achievements in its two big galleries. Most disciplines are well represented, although the country's most popular sport —ice hockey—is conspicuous by its absence.

Understandably enough: you'll find it under the same roof, but reverently showcased in its own right, as the **Hockey Hall of Fame**. This section is something of a shrine to hockey fans, who visit regularly to browse through the memorabilia of masks, skates and hockey sticks—including one used by hockey star Bobby Hull—as well as trophies like the famous Stanley Cup.

On the opposite side of Gardiner Expressway stands **Old Fort York**, holding its own amid zooming traffic and railway tracks. It was once perched right on the lakeshore, but landfill has since pushed the shoreline southward. Constructed in 1793 by Lieutenant-Governor Simcoe, the fort was destroyed by the retreating British in 1813, rebuilt in 1841, and restored in 1934 as a tourist attraction. You can admire some authentically furnished 19th-century officers' quarters, a mil-

*Old Fort York—still under siege, but today's invaders are welcome.*

itary surgery and other historical displays, including a diorama of the Battle of York.

Going back past Harbourfront to the eastern reaches of Queen Street, you arrive at **The Beaches**. Here a lengthy boardwalk, peopled by dog-walkers and joggers, seems to stretch out to infinity along with the sandy beach. The Beaches is fashionably residential and has the expected number of colorful small restaurants and boutiques alongside attractive houses reminiscent of Nantucket. Nearby are Kew Gardens and Greenwood Race Track, where thoroughbred horses run and trotters and pacers prance.

# Heart of Downtown

Bay Street, along which the banks are built like cathedrals, cuts through the heart of downtown. They may not be Chartres, but these latter-day money temples certainly merit attention.

However, some of their elderly neighbors are also distinguished and well worth visiting. **Union Station** is a grand Neo-classical structure with limestone columns and Italian tile ceilings. Built in 1927, its echoing halls are still used as a railroad station, thanks to some militant preservationists, who saved it from the wreckers' ball. The **Royal York** opposite was Toronto's first big hotel. It has hosted royalty and still offers 1,600 rooms, as well as restaurants, nightclubs and a large underground concourse lined with shops. At Church and King streets, the **King Edward Hotel** is another grandiose palace, recently revived to royal splendour, with an elaborately carved atrium, crystal chandeliers, oriental rugs and art nouveau mirrors.

In a more modern vein, the gigantic concrete building at Yonge and Front streets is **O'Keefe Centre**, home to the National Ballet of Canada and the Canadian Opera Company. Next door is the equally important **St. Lawrence Centre for the Performing Arts**, specializing in Canadian drama. A block away, at Jarvis and Front streets, lies the big indoor-outdoor **St. Lawrence Market**—open Tuesdays to Saturdays, but most fun on Saturdays when stalls display an inviting array of snack food and there are busker acts in the streets.

Nearby, **St. Lawrence Hall** is a beautiful mid-19th-century building restored to pink-and-green elegance in 1967; used now by the National Ballet of Canada, it was where P.T. Barnum displayed the midget, General Tom Thumb. In 1851, the year after the hall was built, Jenny Lind—affectionately known as the Swedish nightingale—sang here and enchanted audiences. It subsequently became an integral part of the city's social and business life. It gradually fell out of favor and into disrepair, until its comparatively recent renovation. It is now one of Toronto's finest old buildings.

Of the striking contemporary financial buildings, you **31**

*St. Lawrence Market presents... A mouth-organ impromptu draws a small but enthusiastic audience.*

shouldn't miss the **Royal Bank Plaza**, a glimmering gold mass at the corner of Front and Bay streets that reflects much of the surrounding architecture as well. This creation of Toronto architect Boris Zerafa is actually covered in 2,500 ounces of real gold. Walk inside, and you'll see a cathedral-high lobby and atrium decorated with some thousands of aluminium cylinders, the work of Venezuelan sculptor Jesús Raphael Soto. From all over, the natural light shines in on the ponds, waterfall and lush greenery.

Just to the north, the **Toronto-Dominion Centre,** designed by Mies van der Rohe, is a handsome complex of black glass buildings. The 36-floor IBM Tower, third-highest of the four towers, has a gallery of Inuit (Eskimo) art.

In the next block north is Canada's tallest office building, **First Canadian Place.** One tower is home to the Bank of Montreal, with access through a pleasant green courtyard, complete with waterfall. The second tower houses the new **Toronto Stock Exchange,** opened in 1983. Behind the Exchange Tower, there is a trading pavilion where visitors can observe the frenetic trading from an observation deck. Best

hours are between 10 a.m. and 2 p.m. Besides admiring a magnificent Art Deco setting with monumental art works in the Exchange Lobby, you can also pick up audio-visual information about how stock markets work—if not the latest hot tips.

Most of the main buildings in the area are linked by a veritable labyrinth of underground concourses, including shopping malls, movie theaters and restaurants, a boon when bad weather strikes.

No matter how it's earned, money speaks in Toronto. Two blocks west of the Stock Exchange, on King Street West, is Mirvish territory, part of the empire of Ed Mirvish, the famed tycoon who came from Lithuania and made his riches from discount retailing. Mirvish, who renovated London's Old Vic, earlier restored Toronto's Edwardian **Royal Alexandra Theatre**, and today its exuberant Broadway musicals and other productions play to packed houses. In restored buildings adjacent to the theater are numerous Mirvish-owned family-style restaurants.

**Church Street** has been aptly named for its several churches: the Anglican St. James Cathedral, the United Church's Metropolitan Church and the Roman Catholic St. Michael's

*Say cheese. The choice will be enough to make you smile.*

Cathedral. All are worth a visit for their façades and interiors, in turn-of-the-century style.

On Bond Street, just south of Dundas, the Victorian **Mackenzie House** provides historical interest, with guides in traditional colonial dress. The first Mayor of Toronto, William Lyon Mackenzie was exiled after leading a revolt in 1837 (see p. 18), but he returned later to Toronto and lived in this house until his death in 1861. The interior has been impeccably restored; you can see exhibits of Mackenzie's life, and the hand-operated flatbed printing press on which he turned out his revolutionary newspaper, *The Colonial Advocate*.

An absolute imperative in Toronto is the **Eaton Centre**. More than just a shopping mall, it's a dazzling, grandiose complex of galleries under an arched glass roof, full of greenery, flowering decor and even a flock of floating fiberglass geese.

With such an atmosphere of super-sell, it's all the more startling to look out on the quiet form of **Holy Trinity Church**, huddled in the shadow of the space-age shopping complex. As one of the city's oldest buildings (1847), the church—together with its neighbor, Scadding House, formerly the home of a Toronto churchman —was accorded the dubious privilege of being allowed to remain while the concrete-and-glass Centre sprouted up around them. Holy Trinity Church's twin towers seem almost to have shrunk since the far-off days when they were imposing landmarks for sailors navigating Lake Ontario.

From the Dundas Street entry you can walk through the Eaton Centre on any level, above or below ground, all the way to Queen Street. It's about a 12-minute hike if you put on blinkers and don't stop to window-gaze, buy or have a snack—a near-impossible feat, since everything in these hundreds of shops beckons you to stop. Built in 1975, Eaton Centre is a monument to the merchandising family that for more than a century has followed the motto, "Goods Satisfactory or Money Refunded". A walkway over Queen Street brings you to another traditional department store, Simpsons.

On the northeast corner of Queen Street West and Bay stands **Old City Hall.** Now used to house Provincial Courts, it's a typical Victorian building with a large clock tower, a favorite landmark for Torontonians. Set back on Nathan Phillips Square you'll see the **New City Hall**, designed by Finnish architect Viljo Revell. Completed in 1965, it's a handsome structure with two curved towers flanking a low circular building, reminding many people of an oyster opening on its pearl. Henry Moore's statue of *The Archer* outside attracts some attention. West of the square, **Osgoode Hall** stands out as a lovely golden stone and brick Georgian building. Since 1832 it has been the seat of the Law Society of Upper Canada.

**Campbell House**, on the northwest corner of Queen and University streets, is an exemplary Georgian mansion in red brick that once belonged to Sir William Campbell, Chief

*Working lunch on the move for Toronto's downtown executives.*

Justice of Upper Canada (1825–29). You will be shown around by guides in Colonial Dames' costumes. In 1972, the building was moved here lock, stock and barrel from its original site about 3 kilometers (2 mi.) away.

Northwest of here, around Grange Park, the **Art Gallery of Ontario** on Dundas Street, is a highlight for art lovers (see p. 46). Adjoining the gallery is **The Grange**, an elegant Georgian country house built in 1817 by d'Arcy Boulton Jr. on property that once stretched 3½ kilometers (2 mi.) from Queen up to Bloor Street. Later, an American professor lived in the house and his widow willed it to the Art Gallery.

The house is a microcosm of fashionable life in Toronto as it was early last century, above and below stairs. You can immediately capture the atmosphere of discreet elegance by a tour of the building, which was restored in 1973 to its former color and grace as a typical gentleman's residence of the time. Note the circular cantilevered staircase, stained-glass windows and statuary. What your imagination doesn't furnish, a slide presentation will —with deferential costumed staff carrying out the duties of 36 a century and a half ago.

The English poet Matthew Arnold, describing a visit he had made to The Grange, wrote that in all his travels he had experienced "nothing so pleasant and so home-like".

On McCaul Street, across from the Art Gallery, the **Village by the Grange** has a tempting plethora of boutiques and restaurants in an olde-worlde atmosphere.

As you go further west, the ambience becomes progressively oriental. Toronto's **Chinatown** originally grew up around Dundas and Elizabeth streets, but the construction of high-rises, parking garages and the New City Hall forced it west along Dundas and north up Spadina Avenue. Toronto's Chinatown has all the dragon kites, paper lanterns, herbal medicine shops and odors of exotic spices you'd expect of such a district. Stop at **China Court**, an assortment of Chinese boutiques complete with authentic pagoda roof, garden and bridge.

Turn on to Kensington Avenue for a look at **Kensington Market**, a wonderfully disorganized but amiable street market where jostling crowds of many ethnic groups wander about looking for bargains in everything from toys to tomatoes.

# DOWNTOWN TORONTO

*Shades of suburban England: paintbox villas near Kensington Market.*

## Queen's Park Area

Up wide and pleasant University Avenue, embellished by greenery and statuary, you'll come to oval **Queen's Park**, whose centerpieces are the pink sandstone **Provincial Parliament Building** and other government edifices. Guided tours of the halls and chambers take in exhibits of the development of parliamentary government and displays of Ontario minerals.

On the south side of the park, the curved, mirrored building that catches your eye is the **Ontario Hydro** building, housing offices of the government water and electricity board. It is in itself an eco-

Victorian to modern (signs outside show what the various schools or disciplines are). You can't fail to note the enormous and quite handsome multi-faceted contemporary **Robarts Library**.

A 20-minute walk west of here, on Markham Street, is **Markham Village**, a block of antique shops, bookstores, art galleries and restaurants, housed in Victorian buildings restored by mogul Mirvish. Honest Ed's, between Bathurst and Bloor on Markham, is a curiosity of a discount store opened by Mirvish soon after he arrived from Lithuania. Behind the gaudiness and the punning signs—"Only the floors are crooked!"—there are some good buys here.

logical example, as it is lit and heated from underground thermal reservoirs.

West of Queen's Park is the **University of Toronto**, widely considered Canada's top university and one of the best in North America. Its medical school is renowned, especially since the discovery of insulin here in 1921 by Frederick Banting and Charles Best.

The university buildings represent an assortment of architectural styles from Gothic and

## Yorkville Area

Lying off Avenue Road, **Yorkville** is a great strolling neighborhood, crowded with boutiques and cafés. Once a tawdry hippie hangout, reformed and renovated Yorkville is now almost self-consciously chic, with a well-dressed population promenading around the pretty houses. Cumberland Court and Hazelton Lanes are the most delightful and exclusive malls within the area.

Not far from here, on Yonge, one block north of Bloor, you'll come to the stunning **Metro Toronto Library**, a massive red-brick and glass building designed by Raymond Moriyama, the architect who masterminded the Ontario Science Centre. The interior is breathtaking: a light-filled atrium several stories high, decorated in shades of burnt orange and embellished by luxuriant greenery, a fountain and pond. A plexiglass elevator plies silently between floors.

**The Annex**, a few blocks west of Yorkville, is a more laid-back version of Yorkville, home to intellectuals, artists and "yuppies" (young urban professionals). Naturally, The Annex has its share of restaurants and cafés, movie theaters and art galleries.

North of The Annex, **Casa Loma**, 1 Austin Terrace, is something of a curiosity. Some call it a marvel, others a neo-Gothic monstrosity; whatever you may think, you certainly won't deny it's impressive.

Fascinated by medieval castles, financier Sir Henry Pellatt built the 98-room mansion between 1905 and 1911 at a cost of $3½ million. It took him a number of years just to collect the materials to have Casa Loma built. After examining the construction of old-world castles, he chose his oak and walnut from North America; teak was sent from Asia; and the paneling, as well as marble and glass, came from Europe. Even the huge wall around the 2½-hectare (6-acre) grounds required special treatment —stonemasons were brought across from Scotland to do the job.

With all the terraces, massive walls and echoing rooms, it isn't a cozy folly. But you can admire Pellatt's sense of the grandiose in the paneled Oak Room (which took European artisans three years to complete) and the stained-glass dome, marble floors and Italianate bronze doors of the Conservatory. Peacock Alley, a hall with carved oak walls, takes its name and shape from one in Windsor Castle. If that's not enough, take the 800-meter (2,500-ft.) tunnel from the wine cellar to the stables, where the horses were royally housed in a setting of Spanish tile and mahogany. You can also follow the financier's secret escape-route —a hidden staircase leading from his study.

*Time for a drink at one of Yorkville's sleek sidewalk cafés.*

41

# Toronto's Neighborhoods

The real Toronto is perhaps to be found in its many ethnic neighborhoods, away from the downtown city center. Northwest of Casa Loma, at Dufferin and St. Clair Avenue West, is the heart of Toronto's **Little Italy.** Another nearby neighborhood is **Forest Hill,** bounded by Bathurst and Avenue Road and St. Clair and Eglinton. Forest Hill's population is divided evenly between Jewish and Gentile. There are many beautiful homes in the area.

East of Jarvis Street, toward the Don River, **Cabbagetown** is the memorable name given to an area once described as the "largest Anglo-Saxon slum in North America". It was indeed a cabbage plot for poor British immigrants, and the streets reeked of the stuff. But in the early 1970s, the city authorities started to improve what had become a run-down area. Trendies took note and individuals started renovating houses with fervor. The crumbling heaps became quaint Victorian houses—quarters for artists and actors, hairdressers and yuppies. Boutiques, cafés and pet shops sprang up, and real-estate prices skyrocketed.

At the east end of Carlton Street, the former moth-eaten zoo has been turned into a lively small downtown farm, open to visitors.

Avenue Road, a major artery leading north of town, skirts the buildings of **Upper Canada College.** The board of governors persuaded city authorities to leave this venerable private school standing and divert the highway.

There's no special cachet about the Upper Canada College area—it's just a nice residential part of town. East, beyond Mount Pleasant Road and over toward the Don Valley, **Rosedale** is the residential neighborhood of many of the rich. They live in very large houses on big estates, ensconced behind high shrubbery, fences and trees.

Across the Don River on Danforth Avenue (the eastward continuation of Bloor Street), **Little Athens** is as Greek as Athens' own Plaka, with *souvlaki* restaurants and bouzouki music. The Greeks have cheerfully replaced waves of British, then Italian, post-World War II immigrants, who moved out as they moved up financially.

# Museums

The **Royal Ontario Museum** (affectionately known as the ROM), 100 Queen's Park, was opened in 1912 and is best known for its antiquities from China and its archeological displays.

In the recently inaugurated **Chinese Section**, you'll find beautifully arranged works spanning 4,000 years from the Bronze Age to the establishment of a republic in 1912. This rare collection was gathered mainly by George Crofts, a fur trader and entrepreneur who lived in Tianjin; following his death in 1925 the collection was continued by the Anglican Bishop of Hunan, William Charles White. From snuff bottles of semiprecious stones and models of a Ming tomb and noble house to tomb figures, this fabulous display will thrill you, while excellent captions explain how house plans depended on the elements and seasons, and how the splendidly expressive burial objects related to religion.

The **Bishop White Gallery** is centered on several Buddhist and Taoist Yuan-dynasty frescoes, with outstanding polychromatic and gilt wooden Buddhist deities in larger-than-life size.

There are many other good exhibits, ranging from ancient Egyptian art (along with a mummy) to Etruscan gold objects, medieval silver and European decorative arts.

Upstairs, you won't want to miss the natural history section, especially the **dinosaurs**. Skeletons of these extinct creatures—mainly unearthed in Alberta—are set in recreations of their natural habitat.

There are also excellent dioramas of existing animals. Crustaceans to centipedes all have their place, and the reptile display is enough to chill the blood.

The unmistakeable dome of the **McLaughlin Planetarium** is right next door to the ROM. In the main theater, you can lie back and enjoy a short film about the universe and other extra-terrestrial matters. There are also regular Laser Light Shows.

The **George R. Gardiner Museum of Ceramic Art**, 111 Queen's Park (across from the ROM and opened in March 1984), contains a magnificent collection assembled by financier Gardiner in a mere seven years. Mrs. Gardiner took a special course in London to learn more about prospective purchases and art history. The building cost an estimated $6 million, the collection $16 million. And experts agree that the exhibits are very fine indeed. Not only that, but viewing the collection is also a ceramics course in itself, with the different methods from 2000 B.C. right up to the 18th century carefully documented.

The pre-Columbian displays are exemplary, particularly objects from shaft-tomb cultures. Figures and other earthenware items show a high degree of artistry, despite the fact that they were fashioned without a potter's wheel.

The dazzling display of European pottery contains Renaissance works from the Medici factory. The Italian style of the era is Maiolica —earthenware glazed white with tin oxide and richly decorated with paint taken from metallic pigments. Alongside are 16th- and 17th-century Delftware items—the English equivalent of the tin-glazed earthenware.

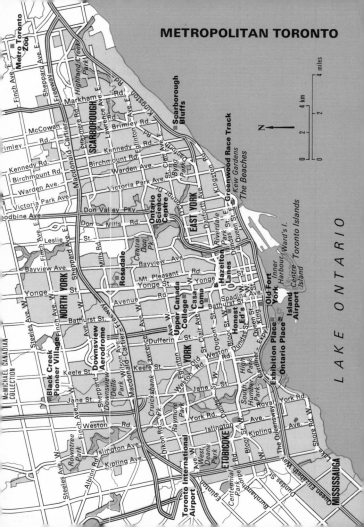

# METROPOLITAN TORONTO

Metro Toronto Zoo

Finch Ave.

Sheppard Ave. E.

Highland Creek

Markham Rd.

Ellesmere Rd.

Lawrence Ave. E.

Kingston Rd.

Scarborough Bluffs

McCowan

SCARBOROUGH

Brimley Rd.

Grimley

Kennedy Rd.

Macdonald-Cartier

Eglinton Ave.

Freeway

Kennedy Rd.

Birchmount Rd.

Birchmount Rd.

St. Clair Ave. E.

Greenwood Race Track

Warden Ave.

Warden Ave.

Byng

Kew Gardens

Victoria Park Ave.

Victoria Park Ave.

Dufferin

The Beaches

Woodbine Ave.

Don Valley Pky.

Ontario Science Centre

EAST YORK

Danforth Ave.

Kingston

Leslie

Don Mills Rd.

Mills Rd.

Riverdale

Gerrard St. E.

Dundas St. E.

Finch Ave.

Sheppard Ave. E.

NORTH YORK

Bayview Ave.

Central Don Pk.

Rosedale

Bayview Ave.

Mt. Pleasant

Hazelton Lanes

Inner Harbour

Ward's I.

Bayview Ave.

Yonge St.

Yonge

Ward's Island

Toronto Islands

Yonge

Avenue

Rd.

Casa Loma

Spadina

Island

Centre Island

Steeles Ave. W.

Bathurst St.

Upper Canada College

Bathurst St.

Old Fort York

Bathurst St.

Island Airport

Downsview Aerodrome

Finch Ave. W.

Honest Ed's

Dundas St. W.

Queen St.

King

Black Creek Pioneer Village

Eglinton Ave. W.

Bloor St. W.

Gardiner Expy.

Exhibition Place

Ontario Place

Keele St.

Keele St.

YORK

St. Clair Ave. W.

Old Weston Rd.

Dupont St.

Macdonald-Cartier

Delfs Park

Downsview

Lawrence Ave.

Cruickshank

Raymore Park

Jane St.

South Humber Park

Royal York Rd.

Ave.

Jane St.

York Rd.

Black Creek

Weston Rd.

Dixon Rd.

Islington

Bloor St. W.

Kipling Ave.

The Queensway

York Rd.

Lake Shore Blvd. W.

Rowntree Park

Finch Ave. W.

Weston Rd.

ETOBICOKE

West Deane Park

Islington Ave.

Steeles Ave. W.

Albion Rd.

Kipling Ave.

Eglinton

Dundas St.

Burnhamthorpe

Queen Elizabeth Way

MISSISSAUGA

Toronto International Airport

Centennial Parforec

Dundas St.

McMICHAEL CANADIAN COLLECTION

L A K E   O N T A R I O

N

4 miles

4 km

2

2

0

0

Europe's answer to oriental porcelain is also catalogued, with articles made in both hard-paste and soft-paste porcelain. Production mushroomed several years after the Meissen factories were set up (1710), when the hitherto secret method of making porcelain became generally known. Harlequin and Columbine are colorfully depicted in scenes from the Italian comedy, the Commedia dell'Arte. Meissen and Worcester porcelain includes items made with a yellow background, a comparatively rare feature because of the difficulty of achieving the color.

Outside the **Art Gallery of Ontario**, 317 Dundas Street West, you are greeted by a pair of brooding Henry Moore bronzes—*Large Two Forms*. And inside, a whole wing is taken up by the **Henry Moore Sculpture Centre**. Opened in 1974, this is the world's largest group of works by the English sculptor, most of it donated by Moore and his wife, who both loved Toronto. More than 600 works are displayed; Moore himself designed the main gallery, using natural light to enhance the monumental casts used for many of his celebrated bronzes.

In a different vein, the **European Collection** is also wonderful. Don't miss the beautiful and truly funny series of proverbs painted by Brueghel the Younger. There are also canvases by Tintoretto, Gainsborough, Rembrandt, Renoir, Gauguin, Picasso and others. You will see a fine collection of late 19th- and early 20th-century sculpture in the **Walker Gallery**.

No less important is the **Canadian Collection**, in an extension. This—one of the most comprehensive collections of Canadian art in existence—traces its development from 200 years ago to the present day. Fine examples of the paintings of the Group of Seven (see p. 52) hang alongside works by contemporary artists. Particularly representative of the landscape styles of the Group are *The West Wind*, by Tom Thomson, and *Above Lake Superior*, by Lawren Harris.

# Around Toronto

## Ontario Science Centre

Ten kilometers (7 mi.) northeast of downtown, at 770 Don Mills Road, lies a dazzling, high-tech palace of marvels nestling amid greenery in a ravine on the Don River Valley. Young and old alike are so eager to play the scientific games that they hardly notice the fabulous building designed by Raymond Moriyama, which takes advantage of, rather than destroys, the natural setting.

All the sciences have their place here, from anatomy to zoology, and you can learn all sorts of things by just standing around and looking. But what attracts most attention is the contemporary, space-age, push-button aspect. People rush for whatever computer games are available; they press dials to look at planets moving

*The science experience—enough to make your hair stand on end.*

in the heavens; or they plug into demonstration equipment to learn something about balance, coordination and energy.

The Centre shows you the marvels of science in a fascinating and often funny way. You can make your hair stand on end by touching 500,000 volts, and see sparks fly 50 centimeters... try a simulated moon landing... lose your shadow... talk to a computer... see a laser burn through a brick... photograph yourself in the dark with a heat camera... whisper anything but secrets into the parabolic sound reflectors and hear it all broadcast to the world. The possibilities are endless.

One important tip: go early and try to avoid weekends. This scientific gym is a hot drawing-card for tourists and Torontonians alike, and the most popular attractions are usually crowded.

## Metro Toronto Zoo

(An hour's drive northeast of downtown; travel east on Highway 401 and exit at Meadowvale Road.) This zoo is every bit as special as it's made out to be: 287 hectares (710 acres) of sheer fun for humans and a marvelous setting for 3,000-odd birds and animals.

You can get around on foot by following various paths marked by different colored footprints (take blue for a fairly quick walking tour of major pavilions in all weathers). Or else the Domain Train, operating year-round, can get you around the Zoo, where animals roam freely. In the summer, you can ride the Zoomobile and get on and off at the stops you choose.

You'll want to visit the beautifully landscaped **pavilions** representing major zoological areas of the world —Africa, Indo-Malaysia, the Americas, Eurasia and Australasia. They all contain fauna and flora of great beauty, typical of their regions. In the near future, the Zoo is hoping to open a Chinese region.

The Zoo is proud to tell you that this is the only place in the world where the natural environment of the animals is virtually recreated. You'll find Florida alligators slithering in the swamps, Canadian beavers grinding their teeth in the ponds and Malayan orangutans scratching themselves in the jungle.

**Littlefootland** brings children into close contact with the more approachable of animals, and audio-visuals help increase individual participation in the "animal geography" experience.

It can be a long day, so take advantage of the picnic tables at the rest stops. Just wandering through the zoo-park area is made even more enjoyable by the streams and ponds that spring from a waterfall in the Americas section. In winter you can even ski from exhibit to exhibit, quite apart from taking lessons in skiing.

*Black Creek's pioneer-style baking: Grandma would approve.*

## Black Creek Pioneer Village

(About 25 minutes by car northwest of downtown Toronto at Jane Street and Steeles Avenue, not far from the modern York University.) From an original farm owned by Daniel Stong in the 19th century, the Metro Region Conservation Authority has built up a lively period-piece village. Authentically costumed guides demonstrate the activities of the time: tilling the land, grinding flour in the

mill, weaving or smithery. From log cabin to "Doctor's House", each residence has its charm, and the country post-house inn where you can enjoy a home-cooked lunch has an anachronistic but welcome touch of air conditioning for hot summer days. Horse-drawn carts or sleighs haul happy kids around, and throughout the year there are parties for harvesting, sheep shearing and other seasonal pursuits.

## Canada's Wonderland
(Not far from Black Creek Pioneer Village; drive north on Highway 400 and take the Rutherford Road exit.) Highlights of this Disney-style park include the Medieval Faire, with a castle, pond, the Canterbury Theatre and a pub; International Street, with pavilions from all over the world offering snacks and boutique wares; the Happyland of Hanna-Barbera peopled with familiar cartoon characters; and Smurf Forest, home to other tiny personalities. The fantasyland is dominated by Wonder Mountain, with water cascading down from its heights.

*A personal welcome to Wonderland from Senior Citizen Smurf.*

Live entertainment runs the gamut from Broadway musical numbers to high diving off the artificial Wonder Mountain. One thrill is a rough raft-ride through White Water Canyon, where nobody minds getting wet on a summer's day. If you do mind, you could always try one of the park's five roller coasters.

## McMichael Canadian Collection
(In the village of Kleinburg, just over half an hour's drive northwest of Toronto; take Highway 400, then turn left along Major Mackenzie Drive). The museum is in a striking native stone-and-log structure in a lush forest overlooking the Humber Valley. Robert and Signe McMichael bought their land in 1952, built a comfortable cabin-house and started filling it with paintings of Canada.

By 1964, so much art had accumulated that the owners decided to show it to the public; the museum was built (with state help) adjacent to the original house in the same style, and today the McMichaels still take a keen interest, although they are no longer permanent curators. The highlight: the largest collection of canvases by the Group of Seven, attractively **51**

## The Group of Seven

The Group of Seven revolutionized Canadian landscape painting in the first half of this century, achieving international recognition. The original "seven" consisted of Franklin Carmichael, Lawren Harris, A. Y. Jackson, Frank Johnston, Arthur Lismer, J. E. H. MacDonald and Frederick Varley. Before World War I, several of them had worked with and been inspired by Tom Thomson, who quit commercial art to paint Canadian landscapes; he died by drowning in 1917, but his followers banded together.

The Group of Seven label was a defensive measure against criticism of these artists' somewhat iconoclastic work, which turned away from the current slavish imitation of European styles, deriving inspiration from personal interpretations of lakes and hills. Rocks, pines, snow and water were presented in new ways, sometimes so schematically that they were almost abstract—particularly in the work of Lawren Harris. The group took in further members and influenced others, including Emily Carr. Although the Group disbanded in 1932, the Canadian landscape-painting movement kept on energetically well into the 1950s.

presented to emphasize various styles and approaches—an outstanding tribute by art patrons to the painters' glorious celebration of the Canadian landscape.

The McMichaels also admire native art. In front of the museum, you are greeted by an impressive soapstone Inuit sculpture of a bear. Indoors are carvings and totem poles, paintings, silver and beadwork.

The museum has a very attractive gift shop and restaurant —and visitors can relax among the pines and make a day of it.

## East of Toronto

At **Cullen Country Barns** (off Highway 401 take Kennedy Road, about 25 minutes from Toronto), a former professional gardener, Len Cullen, has created a magnificent series of naturally weathered barns selling a vast array of antiques, arts and crafts, toys and gifts, with several attractive restaurants scattered around. Torontonians come out here to stock up on plants, trees and gardening equipment.

Len Cullen's first-love project was his **Cullen Gardens and Miniature Village**, about 15 minutes by car east, near Whitby. Open April to October, with Christmas events as well, the Lilliputian village is loved by young and old alike. It boasts old store fronts, farms and swimming pools, a train system, even a scale-model fried-chicken eatery—plus an adjoining miniature amusement park and lake. There's a full-sized restaurant on the premises, as well.

Just over 10 kilometers (16 mi.) east of Whitby is **Oshawa**, known as Canada's Detroit, for here the name McLaughlin is as famous as Ford. From carriages to the McLaughlin Buick, the company pioneered early motor vehicles, until sold in 1918 to General Motors. Today you can see the **Canadian Automotive Museum** at 99 Simcoe Street South, documenting the history of the Canadian automobile industry with wonderful antique cars on display. It emphasizes Oshawa's role in the early years of the industry. Start with the 1898 Redpath Runabout, and work through the 50 fascinating vehicles.

The town's big attraction is **Parkwood**, Colonel Sam McLaughlin's mansion (270 Simcoe Street North), where you can view much luxury and rather erratic taste, as well as wandering at leisure among the trees, statuary and fountains in the splendid gardens.

# Excursions

## Niagara Falls Area

Before becoming part of the 14 million-odd visitors annually swarming around the falls, you may want to stop off at **Hamilton** (pop. 312,000), known as Canada's Pittsburgh for its steel industry. Off Queen Elizabeth Way from Toronto, you can exit to the **Royal Botanical Gardens**, which are spread out over 800 hectares (about 2,000 acres). Highlights are the Rock Garden, the Spring Garden and the superb Rose Garden.

**Dundurn Castle**, off York Boulevard leading into town, is a proud Neo-classical mansion built by Sir Alan MacNab, a rich lawyer, industrialist and politician who was joint premier of the united Province of Canada from 1854 to 1856. MacNab went broke before he died, but the house has been restored to much of its former splendor, with period furniture.

Hamilton boasts an area of well-renovated old houses called Hess Village, as well as a farmer's market and the Art Gallery. All are not far from the City Hall in the center, and well within walking distance of one another.

## Niagara Falls

Coming non-stop from Toronto by car you can reach the falls in about one and a half hours or less.

In spite of honeymooners' hype and commercial gaudiness, the place is still far too awesome to be shrugged off as a tourist trap. The 34 million gallons of water a minute roaring over those limestone cliffs, and the rising white mist, make even the most jaded tourists stop and stare.

The falls were formed after the last Ice Age, as Lake Erie cut a channel into the area below—now Niagara River, once part of old Lake Iroquois. The water continues to erode the escarpment and, unless steps are taken, it is inevitable that the gorge will be cut back completely some day and the falls will flatten out into mere rapids.

The first white man on record as seeing the falls was a French priest, Father Louis Hennepin, in December 1678. He was so enthralled, he estimated the escarpment was 92 meters (302 ft.) high. It is in fact only 51 meters (167 ft.), but the breathtaking sight is likely to fool anybody.

In the last century the falls became a favorite hangout of hustlers selling everything

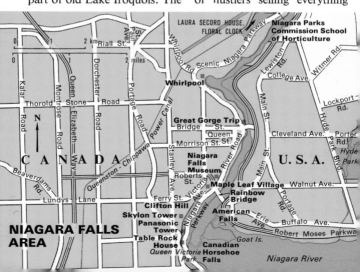

NIAGARA FALLS AREA

imaginable to the gaping sightseers—everything, that is, except the falls themselves. Honeymooning supposedly started when Napoleon's brother arrived with his bride after traveling by stage coach from New Orleans. Today, rapt young couples still pose in front of the falls for a memento photo.

Ontario and New York State purchased much of the land and started to oust the hucksters in the early part of this century. The Canadians made a great success of landscaping their side with vast terraces, gardens and lawns, but commercialism is still around, albeit with a prettier face.

The **American Falls**, facing you as you stand on the Canadian side, are 300 meters (1,076 ft.) wide; the more spectacular Canadian **Horseshoe Falls**, named for their shape, are nearly 800 meters (2,600 ft.) wide. The two are separated by tiny Goat Island, named for its original inhabitants.

You can view the falls from above, beside or beneath. From **Rainbow Bridge**, leading over to the U.S. side, you walk along for a couple of kilometers in the **Queen Victoria Park** area, viewing the American Falls opposite and stopping at **Table Rock House**, perched facing the brink of Horseshoe Falls. Lifts descend to scenic tunnels with portals for viewing the mighty waters from underneath. If you choose this lower vista, avail yourself of the proffered raincoat; it's wet down here. Around Table Rock House are shops and restaurants, as well as many walkways and viewpoints.

The **Maid of the Mist** is a famous boat, named for a legendary Indian girl who was thrown into the falls as "bride of the river". The exciting boat trip up to the booming waters is both deafening and drenching: waterproofs are offered with the ride.

Several **towers** afford a bird's-eye view, including the Minolta and Skylon, both of which bristle with other attractions, such as an aquarium, a glass museum, a revolving restaurant, nearby amusement rides, snack bars and more. The Clifton Hill area offers several museums, with exhibits ranging from hilarious to rather touching: waxworks, the Guinness Museum of World Records and Ripley's Believe It or Not Museum. And on River Road the Niagara Falls Museum contains some irrelevant Egyptian mummies among Indian artifacts and nature exhib-

its. Maple Leaf Village attracts visitors for its restaurant, shopping complex and Elvis Presley Museum.

Downstream along River Rapids Road is the **Great Gorge Trip**, where you descend by lift to view the turbulent rapids and see the **Daredevil Exhibit,** whose name says it all; it pays tribute to all those crazies who made it alive or not over the falls in various conveyances, mostly barrels. One section is devoted to the French tightrope walker Blondin, who made regular trips across the falls on a wire between 1859 and 1860.

From Whirl-a-Port, at Victoria Avenue and Niagara Parkway, you can take a helicopter flight for an overview of the falls. On the Niagara River, the foaming Whirlpool can be seen from a cable car, called the Spanish Aero Car, as it swings 549 meters (1,800 ft.) up over the gorge.

Scenic **Niagara Parkway** heads northeast, with stops at the Niagara Parks Commission School of Horticulture, a model show of colorful flowers in season, and the Floral Clock, which has 25,000 plants and a diameter of 40 meters (131 ft.). Other interesting stopping places include the Georgian-style McFarland House and the Laura Secord House, which belonged to a courageous Royalist who went tearing round to the British troops one night to warn of an approaching American invasion in the War of 1812.

Beyond these attractive parklands with picnic and bathing spots, you'll pass dozens of orchards and vineyards set back from the road. This is Canada's prime fruit-growing region, thanks to the moderating influence of Lake Ontario.

## Niagara-on-the-Lake

Just 29 kilometers (18 mi.) northeast of Niagara Falls, this is undoubtedly one of the most appealing old towns in North America. The first capital of Upper Canada, it was burned down in 1813, but was soon rebuilt in the attractive 19th-century style you see today.

On the way into or out of town, stop off at **Fort George**, the main British outpost of the Niagara frontier in the War of 1812. Leveled by American artillery in 1813 and gradually reconstructed since 1930, it is manned by "soldiers" in British uniform, who show the activities that went on inside the stockade.

Besides historical charm, Niagara-on-the-Lake is famed for the May-to-October Shaw

Festival, which started in 1962 to celebrate the works of George Bernard Shaw, with performances by outstanding Canadian and British casts. Works by other playwrights are also staged.

There are three theaters in all, but the main **Festival Theatre** at Wellington Street and Queen's Parade Road, on the edge of town, is worth a visit, even if you don't have a ticket for a play. A handsome contemporary brick-and-glass structure with a wonderful native wood interior, it also boasts an attractive garden with willow trees and a pond (a perfect setting for intermission drinks).

Shaded Queen Street leads past Simcoe Park, a favorite for picnics, and on to the old Prince of Wales Hotel opposite the distinctive clock tower. A stroll along Queen Street will take you past clapboard and brick buildings with their share of boutiques and ice-cream parlors to tempt you. The **Niagara Apothecary** (1820) sells postcards rather than medicines, but displays the colorful old cases and jars used for the remedies of the time. Carefully restored, the apothecary still has walnut and butternut fixtures, and quaint crystal gasoliers.

# Stratford

This delightful town of 26,000 lives up to its name in every way. Not only does it host the well-known Stratford Festival from May to November, but it also has a quaint and bucolic atmosphere worthy of the Bard's English birthplace—and though the play may be *the* thing, it is certainly not the only thing to enjoy here. Stratford is just over two hours' drive from Toronto, but many visitors like to spend the night here after a late performance.

Shakespeare would probably have approved of the **Festival Theatre's** spiky crown shape, with its commodious, nearly circular seating area and convertible thrust stage. Curtain times are announced by a trumpet fanfare played by musicians in Renaissance bloomers, and between acts the audience can relax with a drink on the terrace. But this showpiece isn't the only theater in town. The Avon Theatre offers traditional charm with a proscenium stage, while the Third Stage features mainly Canadian fare, as well as jazz concerts, throughout the summer.

**Queen's Park**, adjacent to the Festival Theatre, provides a peaceful walking and picnic 59

## Shakespeare and Co.

In 1830, an innkeeper named William Sargint called his hostelry in the area—known as Huronia—Shakespeare Inn, hanging out a sign with a picture of the bard. The small village here officially became Stratford in 1835, and the local river, of course, was called the Avon. In the early 1900s, a Stratford citizen, R. Thomas Orr, pushed the town council into rebuilding a crumbling dam, cleaning out some marshland and creating a 72-hectare (175-acre) park.

*A perpetual midsummer night's dream in the other Stratford.*

The new lake resulting from the dam was christened Lake Victoria.

Fifty years later, a journalist named Tom Patterson conceived the idea of an Ontario Stratford Festival, similar to the English original, and enlisted the help of Sir Tyrone Guthrie.The opening, in 1953—which took place in a tent—was a smash hit. Since then, graced by such international stars as Peter Ustinov and Maggie Smith, virtually all performances have been to a full house. A contemporary theater, designed by John Fairfield, was completed in 1957, and won the Massey Gold Medal for Architecture.

spot for before or after the play. Stratford people are proud of the ducks and graceful swans on Victoria Lake in the park. Over the footbridge in Confederation Park, at 54 Romeo Street, is The Gallery Stratford, with changing exhibitions, some relating to Shakespeare, others contemporary art. If you follow the lake to the dam, you'll find a gate leading to the **Shakespearean Garden**, where you can admire the flowers—those that Shakespeare mentioned in his sonnets and plays—as well as a bust of Shakespeare and a sundial presented by a former mayor of Stratford-upon-Avon in England.

Ontario's Stratford is sparkling clean, graced with turn-of-the-century stone or brick stores. Colorful places to eat include several jolly English-style pubs. Don't miss **The Church**, at 70 Brunswick Street, surely one of the world's most original restaurants. This 19th-century Protestant church was falling into ruin when the present owner bought and converted it. The superb stained-glass, Gothic-style windows, the oak-and-stone interior and big organ pipes make an impressive setting for the French-style buffets, and in the choir loft there's a cozy bar.

# London

London is a medium-sized city of more than 250,000 people, about 40 kilometers (25 mi.) south of Stratford, with a newly renovated Victorian-style center. The city's oldest remaining building, **Eldon House** (1834)—now a historical museum—is furnished just as it was in the period.

Another aspect of life in those days is the **Labatt Pioneer Brewery**, a replica of the original building which shows you how beer was made more than 150 years ago.

The history of Canada's oldest regular infantry force is presented at the **Royal Canadian Regimental Museum**. Highlights are the regiment's roles in the North West Rebellion, the Boer War, the two world wars and Korea.

The **London Regional Art Gallery**, on the banks of the Thames River, is a dramatic modern building designed by Raymond Moriyama. Most exhibits are Canadian, from the 18th to 20th centuries.

There are several open-space areas along the Thames, one of them Springbank Park, which contains a nursery-rhyme-theme section called **Storybook Gardens**. There's a zoo, a miniature train, maze and 63

### Old-Time Religion

The Mennonites are an anachronistic sect related to the Amish or Pennsylvania Dutch in the United States. The sect originated in Switzerland in the early 16th century, and members persecuted for their pacifist beliefs emigrated to the New World. They refuse to serve in the armed forces, and eschew pursuits they consider trivial and unhealthy, such as smoking, drinking, gambling and dancing. The men have long beards and big black hats, the women and girls wear bonnets and pioneer-style dresses. The only mode of travel is horse and buggy. Gentle but withdrawn people, they don't socialize with curious outsiders. However, the Elmira-and-Woolwich Chamber of Commerce gives organized regional tours with discreet views of the farming Mennonites' way of life.

enchanted castle, and you can get there by paddle wheeler, the *Storybook Queen.*

**Fanshawe Park and Pioneer Village,** complete with log cabins, carriage-makers and blacksmith, offers a glimpse of life before the railway came on to the scene. Activities include lake fishing, sailing and golf, with handicraft demonstrations and plenty of wide-open spaces.

You can go further back in time at the **Ska-Nah-Doht Indian Village,** 25 kilometers (15 mi.) west of London on Highway 2. This recreation of a Neutral Indian village of 1,000 years ago has longhouses and a palisade, with special displays and audio-visual presentations.

About 80 kilometers (50 mi.) southeast of London is a landmark in Canadian history—the site of the country's first oil strike just over a hundred years ago, appropriately enough a town called **Petrolia.**

## Mennonite Country

This area of pleasant countryside and villages is the home of the Mennonite community, a strict Anabaptist Protestant sect. Head east from Stratford toward Toronto on Highway 7, which takes you into Kitchener and its twin city Waterloo, perhaps detouring to St. Jacobs and Elmira along your way.

Mennonite life isn't all grim. You can see it at its active best by attending the Farmer's Market in **Kitchener,** which starts at the crack of dawn Saturday morning and continues until

*Charm of yesteryear in the traditional Farmer's Market.*

early afternoon. Here you'll find savory cheeses, sausages, golden apple pies and home-made honey, along with a riot of flowers in season.

Up Highway 85, Elmira and St. Jacobs are small communities surrounded by Mennonite farms, and their typical country stores are well stocked with local crafts.

**Elmira** was one of the first settlements, providing fertile farmland for the Mennonites in the early 1800s. Its quaint stores include Brox's Olde Town Village complex. Harness races are staged at Elmira Raceway, and each year the town celebrates spring with the Maple Syrup Festival, just as the sap is rising in the maple trees.

Tiny **St. Jacobs**—originally called Jacobstettel—has a touch of old-world charm, and you'll find an interesting account of the Mennonite way of life in The Meeting Place Museum.

To the northeast, more commercial than Elmira and St. Jacobs, **Elora** is a fun place to visit. Its arts and crafts shops are in picturesque 19th-century buildings of local stone and wood on the main street, which culminates in an impressive mill-restaurant overlooking the rushing Grand River and falls.

# Georgian Bay Area

The Huronia district around Georgian Bay makes a worth-while day trip from Toronto.

At **Sainte-Marie among the Hurons**, stockades, wood-smoke and costumed pioneer "missionaries" will give you a graphic picture of a remarkable 17th-century French mission.

Watch the film as you go in. Its story is roughly this: in 1639 a group of French Jesuits came to this wilderness to bring religion to the Huron Indians. Aided by the Indians, the Europeans built a peaceful and flourishing community, but it lasted only ten years. Rival Iroquois—jealous of the lucrative Huron-French fur trade—attacked, killing thousands of neighboring Hurons. Then, in 1649, 10 kilometers (6 mi.) from the settlement, two Jesuit fathers, Brébeuf and Lalemant, were tortured to death along with many Hurons. The other Jesuits set fire to their own village as they hastily abandoned it, unable to cope with the savage attack that was bound to ensue. The 300-odd Jesuits returned to Quebec, and contact with the Indians was lost for 100 years.

Today you pass through stone bastions and stockade walls into a carefully reconstructed village. A guided tour is informally given by ebullient costumed students playing the roles of carpenter, gardener, priest and blacksmith—plus, of course, several Indians just being themselves.

You'll see the dirt-floor Church of St. Joseph (now the burial site of the martyred missionaries Brébeuf and Lalemant), the blacksmith's forge, the apothecary's, a tepee and a Huron-style sapling bark longhouse, like the one that was built to make visiting Indians feel at home. Don't miss the handsome **museum** just outside the mission walls— a succession of rooms constructed around a leafy artificial waterfall and woodland indoor courtyard. The exhibits focus on 17th-century France

*Mennonite travel in the 1980s: peaceful and pollution-free.*

*The Jesuit mission: it wasn't always peaceful in Huron country.*

and Canada, with fascinating French objects and Indian artifacts.

A mile or so east, on Highway 21 (on the eastern edge of Midland), you'll see the twin spires of the **Martyrs' Shrine**, a 20th-century monument to eight martyred missionaries, including the Jesuit priests from Sainte-Marie. A pathway uphill leads past bronze reproductions of the Stations of the Cross, and indoors you can view paintings of suffering martyrs or—more pleasantly—vistas of the surrounding countryside.

Across from the shrine, **Wye Marsh Wildlife Centre** provides boardwalks, while naturalist-guides point out the flourishing animal and bird life of the marsh. Wildlife wonders are revealed from an observation tower vantage point or, interestingly, an underwater window. There's also an indoor theater and display hall.

In the town of **Midland**, the Huronia Museum and another faithful copy of a Huron village illustrate the simple lifestyle of the Indians before the coming of the Jesuits. The village has palisades and a firing platform, and the aroma of drying fish. Carry your papoose by wooden cradle board, grind your own corn with round stones, but don't visit the medicine man's lodge if you aren't feeling good. Outside, the fast food on offer in Little Lake Park doesn't smell of woodsmoke.

You might allow time for a boat trip following the route of Champlain, Brûlé and La Salle (see p. 105), although you won't be able to take in more than a few of Huronia's famed 30,000 islands.

Another stop might be at **Penetanguishene** (north on Highway 27) to see the British Naval and Military Establishments. These have been reconstructed in the way they were originally built by the British after the War of 1812, and garrison life is enthusiastically shown by costumed guides, who perform their military duties with zeal.

# Kingston and the Thousand Islands

Main gateway to the Thousand Islands, **Kingston** merits a visit on its own, for its magnificent setting on Lake Ontario (at the point where the St. Lawrence River branches out northeastward) and for its silvery-grey historical houses. In addition, it has the ambience of a university town, for Queen's University, St. Lawrence College and the Royal Military College are all based here, swelling the normal population from 60,000 to nearly 90,000.

First an Indian, then a French-Indian trading post, Kingston became a shipbuilding naval base in the War of 1812. Fort Henry was built in 1832, as the main military stronghold of Upper Canada, and shortly afterwards (from 1841 to 1844) Kingston became the capital of the united Province of Canada.

The many ways to get around include organized short tours, walking and cycling—the latter perhaps the most fun in good weather. You can often rent bicycles in summer, on or near the esplanade in front of City Hall.

Down on the waterfront you can't miss the handsome **City Hall**, with its distinctive dome 69 and weather vane and a big fountain in front—much frequented by young children.

The green esplanade here has several folk-art and craft fairs in summer. Restored, and with a flowered verandah, the old **Prince George Hotel** is currently more student hangout than elegant hostelry, but is still a notable landmark. Behind City Hall, the outdoor weekend **market** on Market Square is a splendid rendez-vous for everyone, from families selling home-grown potatoes or raspberries to aging flower children selling ceramics. The Pumphouse Steam Museum and the Marine Museum are both on Ontario Street near the waterfront.

The most touching historical site is perhaps **Bellevue House**, on Centre Street past Macdonald Park, built like a Tuscan villa as seen by Victorians. Its most famous owner, Sir John A. Macdonald—later prime minister—lived here for only one year, 1848–49, with his dying wife and baby. Restored and furnished in its original style, the house exudes both gentility and sadness, as the guides explain how the household was run, based on Mrs. Macdonald's needs.

Over La Salle Causeway, you might pay a visit to the handsome **Old Fort Henry**, stony and windy on its bluff, and usually lively with student "soldiers" acting out military duties of the last century. Guarded by Martello towers along the waterfront, Fort Henry was never attacked. The **Ceremonial Retreat** is an impressive military show, usually on Wednesday and Saturday evenings in July and August.

Long a holiday playground for Americans and Canadians, the **Thousand Islands** are strung out from Kingston along the St. Lawrence for nearly 80 kilometers (50 mi.). If you try counting them, you'll probably come up with about 1,700—from the merest rocky outcrop to islands big enough for a yacht club or two and a smattering of houses.

If you're not fishing or sailing, you can just sightsee. Several boat lines from Kingston or nearby Gananoque offer day or half-day trips around the islands; the steamboat *Empress* even makes a luxury three-day cruise. The island scenery is striking with dark green conifers and sparkling

*Informal get-together with a majestic city hall background.*

*Get away from it all on the Thousand Islands—there are enough to go around.*

birches set on grassy knolls amid grey and pinkish granite outcrops. Just as interesting are the buildings. Whether simple shacks or rambling mansions, they're all usually dubbed "cottages". Guides point out Millionaires' Row and the places where Irving Berlin, John Foster Dulles, Helena Rubinstein and others came to get away from it all.

Your boat will probably pass under the **International Bridge**, opened in 1938 by Franklin D. Roosevelt and William Lyon Mackenzie King. It required 10,000 liters (2,600 gallons) of light green paint to achieve the artistic color you see now.

**Boldt's Castle** is considered required viewing. You'll find it either a marvel or a spooky Gothic monstrosity, according to your mood and taste. This

## Ottawa

Natural beauty and man-made amenities combine to make the Canadian capital one of the world's nicest. It's a striking sight with its neo-Gothic government buildings overlooking the Ottawa River and green spaces backed by beautiful Gatineau Park. And the cosmopolitan population of 819,000 are a friendly, relaxed group of people.

At the confluence of the Ottawa, Rideau and Gatineau rivers, 195 kilometers (121 mi.) west of Montreal and 395 kilometers (245 mi.) east of Toronto, Ottawa's site was not originally "capital material". Named for the local Ouataouais Indians, the Ottawa River was used by the French for fur shipments to Montreal, and in 1800 Philemon Wright established a settlement here as the key to a waterway route for shipping logs to Quebec. The place didn't attract much attention until Colonel John By came, in 1826, to construct a canal as an alternative to the vulnerable St. Lawrence River. The canal was to be a supply line and troop route between Kingston and Montreal, in the event of an American attack. Construction men and lumberjacks were attracted here, and it

turreted Rhenish folly might have been quite impressive, but it was never finished. George Boldt, the German self-made magnate who owned the Waldorf Astoria Hotel in New York, built it as a gift for his wife. Mrs. Boldt died before the castle was finished, but today troops of delighted visitors wander around the elaborate stone structure and vast, empty rooms to imagine what might have been... perhaps another Waldorf Astoria, by the lake.

soon turned into a rough and roistering frontier-style village known as Bytown, with rivalry flaring between workers from Upper and Lower Canada.

In 1855, Queen Victoria chose Bytown as the capital of the newly formed united Province of Canada. By siting the capital on the borders of Upper and Lower Canada, she hoped that language and other differences could be ironed out. In spite of sniping by the press and others, who considered Ottawa just a brawling backwater, the Parliament Buildings were ready by 1867. The edict was accepted *post hoc*, and the city became a dignified, if somewhat staid, capital, with proper Victorian buildings to suit the new inhabitants. When most of the Parliament Buildings burned down in a terrible fire in 1916, the buildings were quickly restored.

While Ottawa remained nondescript for some years, it burst into bloom during the 1960s, with the arrival of immigrants, an upsurge of patriotic enthusiasm—especially for the 1967 Canadian Centennial celebrations—and new buildings.

Today, it's a wonderful and varied city, boasting top-flight museums and entertainment, good hotels and restaurants —the latter offer a tempting range of national cusines, much as you find in Toronto. All official sights and exhibitions are free.

Although the climate suffers some unfortunate extremes— from wiltingly hot and muggy during part of the summer, to occasional Arctic chills in the winter—in-between weather can be delightful. Gatineau Park, with its seasonal change of color schemes, the blooming tulips in May around the Parliament Buildings and the acres of green space along the canal and rivers make Ottawa truly picturesque.

The sports-minded inhabitants jog and bike all over the place in clement weather, skating or cross-country skiing in winter—often to work. This totally bilingual city (French and English) is a cosmopolitan gathering-place, but those who want a *really* French atmosphere and cuisine cross over the Ottawa River to Hull, just inside Quebec.

In summertime, cheery student guides on bicycle-carts ply central Ottawa to help visitors, and around the Parliament Buildings they are active all year long.

*A proud symbol of Canada: Mountie on guard at Parliament Buildings.*

74

## Parliament Area

The **Parliament Buildings,** on a bluff over the Ottawa River called Parliament Hill, are impressive examples of neo-Gothic architecture, though the Centre Block was largely rebuilt just after the 1916 fire. The 89-meter (291-ft.) **Peace Tower** is topped by a 22-meter (72-ft.) copper spire. Built as a World War I monument, it is notable for its four-faced clock, a 53-bell carillon and an elevator which takes you to the top for a splendid view in all directions.

All tours take in the chambers of the Senate and the House of Commons, and with special permission visitors may sit in on sessions—ask at the tourist office. The highlight of a tour is the majestic **Parliamentary Library**, the one place in the Centre Block not destroyed by the 1916 fire. Lined with its 650,000 volumes, the magnificent pine-paneled room is a 16-sided dome, interesting for its

carvings and also for the imposing statue of Queen Victoria, who rather resembles a Roman emperor. The statue is chiseled out of a solid 12,000-pound marble block. Note, too, the replica of the dome in sugar.

The East Block—the only building to survive the fire entirely—is also open to visitors. Here you'll see four heritage rooms restored to their original 1870s state, including one used by President Reagan during the 1982 summit in Ottawa.

Guard duty is a colorful affair on Parliament Hill, with the RCMP (Royal Canadian Mounted Police) ready to pose on horseback for photos. But the daily **Changing the Guard** in summer (June 24 to Labor Day) is of special interest; 125 red-jacketed, bearskin-topped soldiers of the Governor-General's Foot Guards parade for half-an-hour, from 10 a.m. In the summer, the evening sound-and-light shows illuminate the buildings in fairytale hues for a splendid spectacle.

Cross through the triangular Confederation Square to have a look at the **National Arts Centre**—a handsome concrete

*Cyclists—and fruit—make the best of Ontario's sun.*

complex built in 1969, to the tune of more than $36 million, as a performing arts center, complete with its own restaurant and summer beer-garden by the Rideau Canal. The Tourist Information Centre is on the building's ground floor.

Strolling down adjacent **Sparks Street Mall**, you'll view historical buildings in a pretty, traffic-free setting. There are street vendors and performers to entertain you, and you may well be tempted by the Canadiana, art works and clothing offered in the myriad shops.

A few minutes' walk or ride in the opposite direction (east over the Rideau Canal) brings you to the **Byward Market** area in the Lower Town. After Ottawa was designated capital, this area—named after the canal-builder Colonel By—became a respectable Victorian neighborhood, but fell into dereliction following World War II. It was spruced up for the Canadian Centennial of 1967, and is now considered the popular heart and soul of the city.

Around the market streets you can enjoy quaint Victorian architecture, sidewalk stalls selling everything from exotic spices to gadgets and snacks, or settle down for a full meal in one of the restaurants.

## Sussex Drive

This pleasant route leads through north Ottawa to a beautiful residential part of town. To get in the mood, have a look at the elegant **Chateau Laurier Hotel** (one block from Sussex Drive at Confederation Square and Rideau), a turreted, Victorian-era palace.

Proceeding north along Sussex Drive you'll reach the **Basilica of Notre Dame**, a 19th-century Roman Catholic cathedral remarkable for interior carvings that are painted to resemble stone. Turning on to St. Patrick Street you can drive out through **Nepean Point Park** for a view of the Ottawa River and the 700-seat Astrolabe amphitheater. A fine statue of Samuel de Champlain overlooks the river.

At 320 Sussex Drive, the **Royal Canadian Mint** runs tours to watch coins being stamped and bagged; reserve in advance.

After passing the Lester B. Pearson building, the road crosses over the Rideau River and Green Island, with **Rideau Falls** pouring into the Ottawa River on either side of the island. The windmill you may notice here is part of the Renewable Energy Exhibit, which shows ways of gathering solar and wind energy.

Next is **24 Sussex Drive**, as famous to Canadians as 10 Downing Street is to the British, since this grey stone building, mostly hidden by greenery, is the Prime Minister of Canada's official residence. Just along the road is Government House or **Rideau Hall**, residence of the governor-general.

*Relax on the Rideau Canal, a sleepier side of Ottawa.*

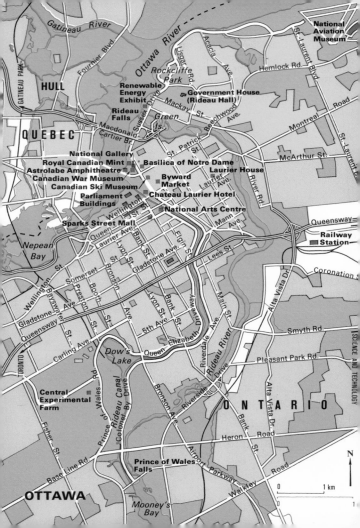

National Aviation Museum

Gatineau River

Ottawa River

Fournier Blvd.

GATINEAU PARK

HULL

Rockcliffe Park

Renewable Energy Exhibit

Government House (Rideau Hall)

Rideau Falls

Sussex Drive

Macdonald Cartier Br.

Green Is.

Mackay St.

Beechwood Ave.

Acacia Ave.

Lisgar Rd.

Hemlock Rd.

Montreal Rd.

St-Laurent Blvd.

Road

St-Laurent Blvd.

QUEBEC

St. Patrick St.

McArthur St.

National Gallery

Royal Canadian Mint

Astrolabe Amphitheatre

Canadian War Museum

Canadian Ski Museum

Parliament Buildings

Basilica of Notre Dame

Byward Market

Chateau Laurier Hotel

Laurier Ave.

Laurier House

River Rd.

Wellington St.

National Arts Centre

Sparks Street Mall

Mann Ave.

Queensway

Wellington St.

Queen St.

Laurier Ave.

Bronson Ave.

Lyon St.

Bank St.

Elgin St.

Gladstone Ave.

Leeds St.

Railway Station

Coronation

Nepean Bay

Bayswater Ave.

Preston St.

Somerset St.

Bronson Ave.

Booth St.

Lyon St.

5th Ave.

Bank Ave.

Queen Elizabeth Driveway

Riverdale Ave.

Main St.

Alta Vista Dr.

Smyth Rd.

Gladstone St.

Queensway

Carling Ave.

Dow's Lake

Queen Elizabeth Drive

Bronson Ave.

Riverside Drive

Rideau River

Pleasant Park Rd.

SCIENCE AND TECHNOLOGY

TORONTO

Fisher Ave.

Central Experimental Farm

Prince of Wales Rd.

Rideau Canal

Colonel By Drive

ONTARIO

Bank St.

Alta Vista Dr.

Road

Base Line Rd.

Prince of Wales Falls

Airport Parkway

Heron Road

Walkley Road

OTTAWA

Mooney's Bay

N

0          1 km

You can drive or walk right in past the guards in British-style uniforms to admire the sweeping stretch of lawns and gardens (open most days, depending on what is happening in the way of receptions). If you obtain special permission, you may be able to visit the mansion.

The drive then makes a circular tour of **Rockcliffe Park**, the exclusive residential neighborhood that also serves as "Embassy Row". The wood, brick or stone mansions are set in manicured gardens with views, and the road circles the RCMP Barracks, where the "show" division of the Mounties trains and gives occasional performances; from here the road winds back to the heart of town.

## More of Interest

If you have time, visit the **Central Experimental Farm**, off Prince of Wales Drive between the Driveway and Base Line Road. Founded in 1886, this 486-hectare (1,200-acre) resident ornamental gardens, an arboretum and showcase livestock.

**Laurier House**, at 335 Laurier Avenue East, is a yellow-brick Victorian structure that served as residence for two prime ministers, Sir Wilfrid Laurier and William Lyon Mackenzie King. The house is shown much as it was when Mackenzie King lived here, displaying even his personal toilet articles, plus many mementoes of his mother and dog—with whose spirits he's said to have communed for advice on affairs of state. While prime minister Lester B. Pearson did not live here, some of his souvenirs on display include an intriguing collection of autographed photos from world leaders.

Across the Ottawa River in Quebec, **Gatineau Park**, a 20-minute drive from the center of town, has much to offer in the 36,000 hectares (88,000 acres) of lakes and woodland, where deer still roam on the remnants of the world's oldest mountain range. Besides hiking and cycling on nature trails or swimming at one of many lakeside beaches, you can also enjoy views from several lookouts and visit **Moorside**, the former country retreat of Mackenzie King. Tea is served in a summer cottage here, and scattered about the grounds are eclectic statuary and ruins brought back by Mackenzie King from his world travels.

To complete or start any Ottawa visit, you may also want

to take a summertime **boat tour** on the Rideau Canal or the Ottawa River, another pleasant way to view the city. Inquire at the Tourist Information Centre.

## Museums

In addition to good, changing exhibitions, the excellent **National Gallery of Canada**, at Elgin and Slater streets, boasts a vast collection of Canadian art and some great European works as well—including paintings by El Greco, Lucas Cranach and later artists: Léger, Gustav Klimt and Picasso.

The National Museum of Man and National Museum of Natural Sciences are both housed in the striking stone Victoria Memorial Building at Metcalfe and McLeod streets.

The **Museum of Natural Sciences**, in the east wing, is an easy-going crash course in natural history from early plankton to recent plants and animals. You can't miss the Dinosaur Court with its handsome model specimens looking natural in their leafy setting on the ground floor. Models of bear, moose and antelope inhabit the second floor, which specializes in dioramas of native Canadian wildlife. Upper floors show elaborations on similar themes.

The **Museum of Man** takes you on a fascinating tour of the evolution of human life in Canada. Look for the "Buffalo Hunters" exhibit, which shows details of the life of prairie Indians, complete with a model buffalo. The "People of the Longhouse" and Inuit exhibits display models of a longhouse and an igloo, along with native tools and art. The "Children of the Raven" shows Indian art at its best, with totem poles, beadwork and other decorative objects.

The **National Museum of Science and Technology**, 1867 St. Laurent Boulevard, gives serious matters a fun-and-games approach. There are views of the heavens through a huge refracting telescope, do-it-yourself demonstrations of balance and optics, and a plastic bubble with live chicks hatching in front of your eyes. In some ways, it's a small-scale version of Toronto's Ontario Science Centre. Unique, however, is the big room filled with old train engines—behemoths from the great era of steam. Another exhibit contains antique cars in mint condition.

The **National Aviation Museum** at Rockcliffe Airport traces the history of aviation, featuring early flying machines, examples from both world wars and the *Silver Dart*—the first plane flown in the British Empire, in 1909. In all, about 100 aircraft are on show, housed in three World War II hangars. You can see wartime planes in action on Annual Aeronautical Day, the second Sunday in June.

The **Canadian War Museum**, 330 Sussex Drive, is filled with memorabilia pertaining to military history, including skulls that Indians took as prizes, a diorama of the Normandy D-Day landings in World War II and Field Marshal Göring's armored Mercedes Benz. Weapons range from Indian clubs wielded during French colonial days to guided missiles and other armaments used today by the Canadian armed forces.

Enthusiastic skier or not, you should take a look at how they did it 150 years ago, at the **Canadian Ski Museum** (457a Sussex Drive). Along with the early contraptions used, other exhibits include changing fashions in ski gear, and even ancient cave drawings. The museum shows the development of skiing, particularly in Canada, in photographic form, with most of the participants the right way up.

You'll find more than 20,000 stamps in Ottawa's **National Postal Museum**, at 365 Laurier Avenue West—most of them Canadian and British North American. The collection follows Canada's postal history from 1604, with displays and dioramas. There are also items from more than 100 other countries.

Further special-interest exhibitions include the **Museum of Canadian Scouting** (1345 Baseline Road), which traces the spread of scouting in Canada and tells the life story of Lord Baden-Powell; and the **Currency Museum**, in the 12-story Bank of Canada building at 245 Sparks Street. This shows how people made out before the first coins were struck, and goes on to illustrate the progress of Canada's currency.

## Outside Ottawa

**Upper Canada Village** is the ultimate showpiece in a country that loves to recreate and dramatize the pioneer past. Located to the east of Morrisburg, 77 kilometers (48 mi.) southeast of Ottawa, it is a beautiful old town, reconstructed when its former location was flooded to create the St. Lawrence Seaway.

In a peaceful, green canalside setting, enlivened by cheeky Canada geese, you'll find authentic pre-1867 buildings, from the timbered sawmill to **83** the brick-built **Chrysler Hall**, which is beautifully proportioned in true Greek-revival style. Lots of real work is being done by people in period costume: depending on when you arrive, you'll see plowing and sowing, weaving and bread baking, and many more traditional activities. At **Willard's** **Hotel** you can enjoy a homespun hot meal or salad lunch, served by waitresses in colonial dress. There are stagecoach and boat rides, and you can climb the small **fort tower** for a good overall view, or look in at the old schoolhouse to see how they used to teach the "three Rs".

*The pioneering spirit lives on in Upper Canada Village.*

# What to Do

## Sports

Sports-mad like all Canadians, almost all Ontarians participate in an active sport of one kind or another—or at least go to watch someone else doing it. Look out of your hotel window to see hordes of joggers and cyclists in the city streets. Hotels often provide full fitness facilities, as well as swimming pools. Athletic and sports equipment is for sale or hire in several shops in Toronto (especially around Bloor Street) and in Ottawa.

### Participant Sports

A bonanza of courts, both public and private, make it possible to play **tennis** without hassle. There are also resorts with excellent tennis facilities, especially around the Muskoka Lakes area. Inquire through the Canadian Tennis Association, 333 River Road, Ottawa, K1L 8B9. The Toronto Office, 25 Imperial Street, Toronto, Ontario M4P 1B9, will give information by phone (416) 488-5076).

There are more than 400 **golf** courses around Ontario, 47 of them in or near Toronto. Glen Abbey, west of Toronto, offers a championship challenge in a beautiful setting, but many pleasant and less rigorous courses are open to the public. Private clubs are usually quite accessible, especially during the week (if you can prove membership of a golf club at home, you can obtain special privileges). Inquire through Ontario Travel, 900 Bay Street, Toronto, Ontario M7A 2E5.

No need to go on about it; Toronto and Ottawa get hot in summer, and there's no lack of **swimming** spots, from hotel and public pools to the beaches of the Toronto Islands, and elsewhere in countless lakes and among the Thousand Islands.

All that water—the Hudson Bay, hundreds of freshwater lakes, the Great Lakes and the Thousand Islands—offers exciting and adventurous **sailing**. You can even learn the sport in excellent schools in Ontario. For yachting and sailing information, contact the Canadian Yachting Association, 333 River Road, Ottawa K1L 8B9.

**Windsurfing** is also very popular, and sailboards are readily for rent around The Beaches area of Toronto, as well as at most lakeside resorts.

In winter, the **cross-country skiing** is superb, with trails around Toronto's ravines and out into the lake, as well as a big network all around Ottawa —not to mention resort-area trails and scenic uncharted tracts all over the province.

**Downhill skiing** is big in Canada, the best areas being in the Far West and in the Laurentians of Quebec. Ottawa offers a good complex at nearby Ski-O, several ski centers that are pleasant without being world class.

**Ice skating** can actually be a means of getting around, especially in Ottawa, where people zoom up and down Rideau Canal during winter freezes. For those who just want to try a pirouette or two, Toronto has many rinks—including one at Nathan Phillips Square outside City Hall and others at College Park (Yonge and College streets) and Kew Gardens.

**Fishing** in the wilderness means just that—you can cast your line without another angler in sight. But you can also fish within Metro Toronto (where there's a "million-dollar contest" for stocked salmon) and Ottawa. All over Ontario are log-cabin resorts where you can relax and exchange fishing stories. Hiring of a boat and guides is easy everywhere. Besides bass, walleye pike and trout, the coveted freshwater catch is the muskellunge or

Photo: Courtesy of Joe Kowalski, Wilderness Tours.

muskie, a daredevil fish of the pike family that often outsmarts the fisherman, and can reach up to 20 kilos (50 pounds). There are strict license requirements, bag limits and seasons.

All over Canada you can go **hunting**, with everything from bow and arrow to rifle, but with strict limitations to regulate the bird and animal population without endangering it.

Bird-hunters flock to Ontario in the fall for partridge,

grouse and woodcock, not to mention the superb geese, which migrate in late September. Guides with dogs are available in some places, although many Americans bring their own bird-dogs. Hunting in Canada doesn't require matched Purdeys or fancy clothes, as it might in Europe —only sporting behavior and good manners.

In the late fall and winter, there's big game to be bagged: whitetail deer, caribou, moose

*White-water rafting: for those who like doing it the hard way.*

and black bear. In the wilds of the north, the Objibway Indians are seasoned guides.

For more information on huntin', shootin' and fishin', inquire at the Wildlife Branch of the Ministry of Natural Resources, Queen's Park, Toronto M7A 1W3.

**Hiking**, **canoeing** and **rafting** provide endless possibilities for exploring Ontario's forests, lakes and rivers. Particularly breathtaking, literally, is white-water rafting on the Ottawa River. For locations, guides and equipment hire, inquire through the Ministry of Tourism, Queen's Park, Toronto M7A 1W3.

*They're at home in Toronto—the Blue Jays of baseball fame.*

"Dude ranch" is the preferred style of **horseback riding** available all around Toronto and Ottawa and in the country and forests, though dressage is taught in some places as well.

## Spectator Sports
**Ice Hockey** is *the* national spectator sport, and children learn it as a matter of course. The Toronto Maple Leafs (members of the National Hockey League) play home-based matches regularly from October to April.

**Curling** usually proves to be a relaxing sport to watch, especially if you have a warming drink beside you. From late fall to early spring, The Terrace (70 Mutual Street) provides a glass-fronted grandstand view for spectators.

**Baseball** gets a big play in Toronto: firm favorites in Toronto are the Blue Jays of the American League East.

**Football** is played by Canadian rules on a 110-yard field (longer than the 100-yard U.S. version) under the auspices of the Canadian Football League, whose great annual event, the Grey Cup, is hotly disputed in an east-west confrontation. Big-league home teams are The Argonauts (CFL football).

**Soccer** has become a popular sport in recent years, particularly at the amateur level. Toronto's soccer team is the Toronto Blizzard (North American soccer).

**Lacrosse** is a truly Canadian sport, although enthusiasm is less ardent than for ice hockey or baseball. Semi-pro games are regularly played in Toronto.

There are important **horse-race** meetings at least four times a year at Toronto's Woodbine Race Track, and several races (flat and harness) at the Greenwood Race Track.

# Shopping

It's true. Toronto really *is* a shoppers' paradise. From one end of the city to the other you can stroll in department stores, boutiques or in underground malls. It's not only an easy pastime (and you don't *have* to lighten your pocketbook), but with the low-key and cheerful approach of both salespeople and customers, it is usually a lot of fun. Most stores accept credit cards, and be sure to ask about a refund (on the provincial tax) if you are taking the goods abroad.

### Where to Shop

You won't want to miss the beautiful, glassy pavilion setting of Toronto's Eaton Centre, at Yonge and Dundas, which is joined by a glass walkway to Simpsons, another famous old retailing name. At Eaton's you can find a variety of wares from a wide choice of fine wines to all sorts of jewelry, men's and women's wear, books and leather goods. Another good bet over- and underground is the famous Hudson's Bay Company at Bloor and Yonge. Fur and leather goods are specialties, but in the mall you'll find just about everything.

At the foot of York Street is **89**

the Queen's Quay Terminal, an old green warehouse that has been transformed and now houses two levels of restaurants and boutiques, a theater, and pricey condominiums. Across the street at 222 Queen's Quay West, is the Harbourfront Antique Market crammed on several floors with clothes, antiques, gifts and much more.

The Labyrinth is a massive system of underground shopping concourses soon to be connected with the Eaton Centre many blocks north. Main entrances are from three big hotels—the Royal York, the Westin and the Sheraton Centre—and directions are posted. This kind of shopping is an obvious convenience during the hard winter.

Queen Street West is a trendy boutique area, with way-out or conventional clothes, health foods, art galleries and bookshops galore. The Village by the Grange, on McCaul Street to the north, has boutiques selling clothes and works of art. West on Dundas, Chinatown displays its own wares, plain and fancy. And nearby Kensington Market offers the bottom-line price range in all sorts of goods.

Yonge Street from Dundas up to Bloor has become known as the "Strip" and used to tout a lot more porn than it does since a recent clean-up. There are several discount houses, and camera and hi-fi shops often provide good buys.

Bloor Street between Avenue and Yonge is the ultimate in luxury shopping, comparable to New York's Fifth Avenue or Paris's rue du Faubourg Saint-Honoré. This is where you head if you can't live without a new Cartier watch, Yves St. Laurent jacket or Gucci bag. Even the people living on the street are somewhat awed by the prices.

Yorkville, just north of Bloor along Cumberland Street and Yorkville Avenue, has its own chic shopping flavor. Fashions are not always conventional or classic, but boutiques are invariably fun, sometimes displaying good clothes by new Canadian or Japanese designers. In these pretty, converted Victorian town houses you'll find everything: art galleries, antique and china shops, scents and soaps, zany gift and greeting-card shops. Don't miss the elegant offshoots here: Cumberland Court and Hazelton Lanes.

*Shopping at Eaton Centre is out of this world.*

Two other areas with a profusion of good little shops include The Annex, west of Yorkville, and in the other direction (around Parliament Street) Cabbagetown.

Markham Street is another great shopping area, specializing in antiques, art and books.

**Ottawa** has its share of good shopping, with seven areas of particular interest:

Sparks Street Mall—five blocks of open-air pedestrian shopping mall, its color and bustle heightened in summer by flowers and street musicians.

Byward Market—the traditional farmer's market, with fresh produce brought in as it always has been, and crafts and antiques also on sale.

Bank Street Promenade—a relaxed shopping walkabout in one of the city's oldest thoroughfares.

New Rideau Centre—a three-level mall containing over 200 stores and services, all air-conditioned.

St. Laurent Shopping Centre —more than 100 stores and services with the accent on fashion.

Glebe Merchants Association—nearly 50 stores and restaurants on Bank Street.

Place de Ville—underground shopping for when the weather turns bad.

**Canadian Specialties**
Contemporary arts and crafts produced by Canadians—often the Indians and Inuits—can be excellent buys. Stores and small galleries all over Toronto and Ottawa are filled with good choices for those who keep their eyes open. Exuberantly colored Indian paintings, wood and soapstone carvings and the like make wonderful souvenirs. Beaded belts, moccasins, jewelry and accessories are also good buys.

Less folkloric but still interesting are elaborately hand-knitted sweaters, hand-painted silk scarves, cotton goods such as aprons, new or old quilts, and fancy, hand-finished throw pillows. Another Canadian specialty is semiprecious stones in jewelry or other objects. Amethysts are well worth looking at, as are items in agate, quartz or onyx.

Furs and leather goods are traditionally Canadian, and come in all qualities and price ranges.

Gift shops galore include all the amusing junk you might want—from Niagara Falls, for instance. But even the falls area has high-quality gift and art shops. Most museums offer excellent wares, as do historical sites. Outstanding are the McMichael Canadian Collection northwest of central Toronto and the Cullen Country Barns at Milliken, northeast of Toronto. Both excel in the choice of attractively presented locally made wares, including Inuit carvings, brass candlesticks, scented candles, embroidery, patchwork quilts, ceramics, toys and much else. There are craft shops in Mennonite country, particularly in Elora, Elmira and St. Jacobs.

*A touch of Montmartre in a Toronto park.*

# Entertainment and Nightlife

Something is *always* happening in both Toronto and Ottawa, from simple street busker acts to full theatrical performances.

Concerts go on year-round. The late Toronto pianist Glenn Gould gave great impetus to all kinds of **music** from Bach to bop. Chamber music is a big attraction in all manner of settings, including "après-brunch" at Toronto's Harbourfront. Roy Thomson Hall is home base for the Toronto Symphony, as well as the famed Toronto Mendelssohn Choir.

Massey Hall hosts both symphonic and jazz orchestras. The Canadian Opera Company—with its special reputation for excellence in performing Handel works—is usually found at Toronto's O'Keefe Centre in the winter. Pop and jazz flourish in Toronto and Ottawa. Toronto is also Canada's **dance** capital, attracting top international stars who perform with the excellent National Ballet of Canada, also based at the O'Keefe Centre.

Top-flight performances of everything from symphony to opera and theater are held in Ottawa at the National Arts Centre.

The Ontario ethnic mix means you might hear anything from Latin-lover music to rock, from the German tuba band to plaintive Hungarian violins. In the summer, small towns and resorts are often the scene of native Indian dancing, folk dancing or do-it-yourself to whatever music is available.

Ontarians love the **theater**. Most productions are in English, and these run the gamut from state or province-subsidized theaters—where first-run ticket prices are quite reasonable—to avant-garde productions in experimental playhouses. Stratford (see p. 59) is as famous on the North American continent as its English counterpart, not only for the classics of Shakespeare but for other genres including jazz and musical comedy. At Niagara-on-the-Lake (see p. 58) the plays of George Bernard Shaw are the centerpiece of the summer festival, but works by many other playwrights are performed as well.

You'll find a huge choice of **movies**, including all sorts of festivals on various themes, such as mystery, women's films, and so on. To avoid line-ups, many theaters allow you to reserve seats in advance.

Informal after-dark activities vary from top-flight cabaret entertainment in Toronto to low-key but enthusiastic piano bars in small-town hotels and resorts. Full-scale floor shows spring to life after dinner in some Toronto hotel restaurants and nightclubs; other restaurants sparkle with live combos or strolling musicians.

In both Toronto and Ottawa, discotheques are lively and informal, and you don't need to know the owner or the password to enter, but you do need money or a credit card.

All over Ontario, midnight or before is usually the end of revels. Even in Stratford, they're thinking of jogging or tennis the next morning.

*In the mood... Singalong at a Kensington Market guest house.* **95**

# Festivals

Ontarians find any excuse for a celebration. Here are just a few of the dozens of special events throughout the year. The dates are best checked with the local tourist office.

**Muskoka Winter Carnival** in early February features crazy winter sports competitions, such as "snow golf", in Bracebridge and Huntsville.

**Winterlude** is Ottawa's big-freeze festival, also in February. Centered on the Rideau Canal, there is skating and ice hockey, with snow sculpture and cross-country marathon skiing.

Ottawa's **Festival of Spring** in late May is a colorful contrast, with four million tulips, fireworks, a flea market and a marathon.

Niagara Falls celebrates spring with a **Blossom Festival**, sporting events and vintage car rallies in late May.

A **Mennonite Charity Sale** takes place in late May at New Hamburg, with brunch, dinner and handicrafts on sale.

**Metro International Caravan** is a nine-day ethnic festival with 60 nations providing food, drink, dance and entertainment all over Toronto at the end of June.

On Lake Superior, Thunder Bay's **Round-Up** celebrates the *voyageurs'* (French fur traders) arrival at Fort William, with a canoe festival and racing, early in July.

**Festival Ottawa**, throughout July, marks the nation's birthday, with regattas, concerts, theater, music, dance, art and craft exhibitions.

Toronto's **Caribana** (see photo opposite) is a weekend of West Indian dance, music and parades, in late July or early August.

Early in August, Mosport's **Can-Am Race** is an endurance test for racing cars.

In the **Six Nations Indian Pageant,** held at about the same time, the Iroquois play out their history in an outdoor amphitheater at Brantford.

The **Canadian National Exhibition** in Toronto is huge, old and ever popular, with crowds flocking to see the livestock, high-tech exhibits and firework displays every night for two weeks at the end of August.

Kitchener's **Oktoberfest** is the drinking event of the year. Early in October there are nine days of German beer, food, music and dance, culminating in a huge parade.

**Fête**, a two-week arts festival, is staged in Ottawa during the first half of October. The celebration takes in visual arts and crafts, theater, dance, music and poetry reading.

# Wining and Dining

The foreign communities have livened up the food scene considerably and turned it from a largely meat-and-potatoes affair into a colorful cosmopolitan pot-pourri. A veritable worldwide gastronomic tour awaits you in Toronto, where there's scarcely a national cuisine that you can't savor. Canadian specialties are still around, however, and among these you can sample wild rice, maple syrup, corn bread, excellent fish, smoked sausage and bacon or rich apple pies.

## When to Eat

**Breakfast**. This is usually served from 7 to 11 a.m. Customarily starting with juice or fruit, it may be limited to a continental-style menu of toast, croissants, doughnuts *(beignets)* or muffins with butter and jam, coffee, tea or hot chocolate. Or it may expand to a big meal of cereal, waffles or pancakes with maple syrup, eggs, sausages or the great Canadian back bacon—a particularly savory type of smoked pork. Fish and steak may be available as well; the lumberjack traditions live on.

**Brunch**. In many restaurants and snack bars, breakfast merges into the special weekend institution: brunch. This may run well into the afternoon, and be accompanied by something stronger than tea or coffee—such as Bloody Marys or white wine. Among the excellent brunch dishes are bran-raisin or molasses muffins, various forms of quiche, eggs benedict (Canadian bacon, poached egg and *sauce hollandaise* served on an "English muffin"), smoked trout, a fabulous choice of vegetable and fruit salads, flavored or plain yoghurts, sandwiches, cold chicken, meat pâtés, hot casserole dishes, and much more, including tarts and other desserts.

**Lunch**. The midday meal may be anything from a sandwich, hot dog or hamburger eaten on the run to an elaborate continental-style meal. Serving usually begins around noon and lasts until 2.30 p.m.

**Dinner**. This is the festive meal, and serving lasts from about 6.30 or 7 p.m. until 10.30 or so. Preceding dinner, cocktail time—or happy hour as it is known—is as sacred as in the States.

*Eat in or take out, fast food often fits the bill in Toronto.*

## Where to Eat

The kaleidoscope of choice—running alphabetically from Argentine beef to Zen macrobiotic—excites even jaded palates. Eating places range from simple and amusing sidewalk cafés up to the grandest establishment, hopefully with food to match the setting and price.

Service everywhere is polite and helpful.

**Fast food** is here to stay, with familiar chains offering up the usual calibrated fare. More fun are the Jewish **delicatessens** and take-out shops, where you can buy a picnic of ready-made sandwiches or fresh salads "to go" in little plastic boxes.

"Delis" also offer favorites like blintzes (thick pancakes, usually with cream), smoked salmon (lox), bagels (special bread), cream cheese, chicken soup and pastrami—savory smoked beef.

**Crêperies** and **waffle houses** serve just what the names suggest, with different types of stuffing and dressing—try drenching your waffles in that Canadian maple syrup.

There's been a revival of the old English **pub**, serving favorites such as steak and kidney pudding, shepherd's pie and ploughman's lunches of cheese, bread, salad and pickle relish. **Wine bars** offer salads and hot food along with a large choice of imported or local wine.

**French** restaurants abound, but of course vary in quality. You'll find old favorites like *foie gras* (goose liver), *tournedos sauce béarnaise* (steak with béarnaise sauce) and *gigot d'agneau aux champignons* (leg of lamb with mushrooms). But watch out for some interesting so-called *nouvelle cuisine*: *saumon frais à la ciboulette* (raw salmon with chives), *lapin sauté à la crème d'estragon* (rabbit with tarragon-cream sauce) or *ris de veau à l'orange et poivre vert* (sweetbreads with a sauce of oranges and green pepper).

**Italian** restaurants are popular and usually good. Besides the usual *antipasti* (starters), various pasta and *prosciutto con melone* (raw ham with melon), you may try *carpaccio* (slivered raw beef with spicy sauce), *scaloppine aurora* (veal scaloppine sautéed with mushrooms and tomatoes) or *involtini di pollo* (chicken stuffed with cheese and ham in cream with mushroom sauce).

Oriental cuisines are well represented, especially **Chinese** and all its regional variations. From Peking comes the favorite Peking duck and barbecues. Szechuan cooking is usually hot and spicy; Cantonese food is milder, with specialties such as chicken with almonds or sweet-sour shrimp.

**Japanese** restaurants feature the usual restrained and elegant decor and food, including *sushi*, *sashimi* (raw fish platters, the former rolled with rice) and lightly fried shrimp-vegetable *tempura*.

**Thai** and **Korean** cooking offer delicate and hot surprises, while **Indian** food includes all sorts of curries, as well as *tandoori* specialties cooked in an earthenware oven.

There are also German, Hungarian, Greek, Turkish, Mexican and Moroccan restaurants in Toronto and Ottawa.

### Sandwiches

These are much as you'd find in the U.S.: tuna (tunny), ham, cheese, egg or chicken salad, roast beef (on all sorts of bread), or club-style—chicken, tomato, bacon and lettuce on toasted layers of bread—plus much more, including "deli" styles and Greek pita bread sandwiches with all kinds of fillings.

### Soups

These can be anything from consommé to turtle, fish, vegetable, *vichyssoise*—the chilled American version of the old French leek-potato soup—or *gazpacho*, the spicy cold Spanish-Mexican tomato-based soup.

### Salads

These are often served at the beginning of a meal, or they may be the main course. As well as simple lettuce and to-mato, there are chicken, egg or spinach and mushroom with garlic-flavored Italian dress-ing. Chef's salad usually con-sists of cheese, ham, tomato and chicken. *Salade niçoise* includes tomatoes, olives, an-chovies, tuna and perhaps green peppers and hard-boiled eggs. Waldorf salad means you'll find slices of apple, celery and nuts in the mixture.

Fish and shrimp salads are usually fresh. Dressings can be oil-and-vinegar Italian (garlic-flavored), thousand island (mayonnaise, ketchup and chopped hard-boiled egg) or blue cheese (Roquefort).

The "French" dressing may be sweet; watch for this in other dressings, since the U.S. taste for sweetness has now reached Canada.

### Appetizers

You'll find all sorts of excit-ing cosmopolitan first courses: fish, liver, meat or vegetable pâtés; quiches of all flavors —including spinach, cheese, egg and ham, crab or salmon. *Escargots* (snails) are usually served in their shells, but may also appear in pastry shells; the Russians serve stuffed pastries called *pirozhki* and *blini* with smoked salmon and sour cream; the Italians offer *anti-pasti* such as marinated veg-etables and thin-sliced Parma ham (*prosciutto*). Stuffed avo-cados or tomatoes appear on many menus, along with much, much more...

### Seafood

It exists in abundance and is usually fresh. Top shellfish items are clams and oysters, either served raw or cooked with a sauce. "Rockefeller" clams **101** are cooked *au gratin* with spinach purée and *sauce hollandaise*. Find an oyster bar if you want to knock back the fresh bivalves off the half-shell and wash them down with beer. There are also wonderful ways to eat scallops, shrimp, crab meat and lobster from the east coast—pricey here as elsewhere. Nova Scotia salmon is a treat, smoked or grilled with melted butter. Many gourmets dote on Arctic char, a delicious white fish. Cod, flounder and halibut can be excellent.

Among freshwater fish, you can hardly go wrong with trout, almost always fresh and sautéed with or without sliced almonds *(amandine)*; up in the lake country you're likely to see fresh perch, pike, bass, or maybe even muskie (a pike-type fish) on menus.

### Meat and Vegetables

Hearty eating is still favored in Canada, and the steak—usually from Alberta—is very good. There are all cuts of beef, including English-style roast beef with Yorkshire pudding, barbecued and broiled steak fillets, T-bones, *entrecôtes* and even *steak tartare* (chopped raw beef with capers, onion, mustard and raw egg) or Italian-style *carpaccio* with various dressings.

Veal may be served grilled with lemon or cream of mushroom sauce, or cooked with cheese and ham (known as *cordon bleu*). Lamb can be excellent in all its forms—rack or saddle, chops or stew. Roast leg of lamb is often accompanied by the traditional mint jelly or sauce. Chicken and turkey, pork, veal and calf's liver turn up in various forms.

Canadians like game and treat it with respect. Duck is available most of the time on many menus and may be served grilled, *à l'orange*, with cherries or even with rhubarb sauce. In the fall, pheasant, quail and venison appear on tables with all sorts of garnishings and sauces. Accompaniments may be delectable corn fritters or wild rice—a Canadian delight coveted even by Paris gourmets these days. Not really rice, it's a grain harvested from marsh grass in swampy areas, a difficult job that makes it a relatively expensive treat.

Vegetables come in many guises in Ontario. Apart from French fries, the U.S. influence has also introduced baked potatoes with sour cream and chives, and France has contributed myriad ways of serving potatoes, including *lyonnaise* (baked with milk or cream). You'll discover all sorts of ways to eat tomatoes, corn (maize), green beans, white haricot beans, snow peas, broccoli, artichokes, baby marrow or zucchini, spinach, peas, cauliflower and celery.

## Cheese

French restaurants offer the best assortment, but nearly all restaurants have various creamy white cheeses, including camembert or brie, or with garlic or herbs, plus Cheddar, Liederkrantz, Münster, Gruyères and Edam.

## Desserts

They're varied and appealing enough to corrupt the most fanatical of weight-watchers. But the area around Lake Ontario is a great fruit-producing region, and low-calorie delights in season include luscious strawberries, raspberries, melons, pears, peaches, apricots, blueberries, plums and apples. From abroad there are bananas, kiwis, kumquats and passion fruit.

Excellent ices, sorbets and ice-creams come in dozens of

*Twilight on the terrace, with a relaxing drink to round off the day.*

flavors, simple and unadorned or with chocolate, fruit and nut sauces, or whipped cream toppings. Health-minded eateries offer delicious frozen whipped yoghurt, plain or with natural flavors.

Pastries range from the most extravagant French goodies (such as éclairs and Napoléons, or more *nouvelle cuisine* articles like kiwi tarts) to native North American pies with short-crust pastry—deep-dish apple, pumpkin, pecan, walnut or mincemeat (especially good around Thanksgiving and Christmas). Lemon chiffon pie is light and the cheesecake can be excellent: it's made with eggs, cream or cottage cheese plus lemon flavoring, and is often served with a fruit glaze or sauce. Fruit or chocolate mousses make light desserts, as does *zabaglione*, the popular Italian confection of egg whipped and warmed with sugar and marsala or white wine. Chocolate freaks can usually find versions of the layered Black Forest cake, often with a rich vanilla custard on the side.

## Drinks

All alcoholic beverages are available, including popular and fancy cocktails in most bars and cocktail lounges. Canadian whisky (rye) is excellent—although it may take a little getting used to—and less expensive than imported whiskies. All alcoholic drinks, including wine, are very expensive—even in the shops—since there is a heavy provincial tax on them.

Wine lists vary. You'll find some places offer simple "house" wines by the glass or carafe, while other restaurants stock some great French vintages. Ontario produces wine in fruit-growing country near Niagara-on-the-Lake, although so far they can't quite compete with better French, Italian or even Californian wines. The drier Canadian whites are quite acceptable, however.

Canada is a beer-making country, and besides imported brands, you'll find the local and excellent labels such as Labatt's, Molson and O'Keefe. Good Canadian apple juice and cider are available as well. Besides the usual soft drinks, restaurants also stock Canadian and imported mineral water.

Tea is popular, and tea-time is still sometimes observed as a ritual. Coffee quality varies. You might have to brew your own in many hotels and other dining places. Many places pride themselves on very good coffee.

## Sailing with Champlain—A Floating Diversion on Ontario's Backwaters

*Even Samuel de Champlain recognized a good tourist attraction when he saw one.*

*The French explorer wrote enthusiastically of the scenic tranquility as his boat drifted through the succession of lakes and rivers laced together northwest of Toronto.*

*This same quietly flowing waterway network soon became a much-needed trade route, linking Lake Ontario with Georgian Bay. Today, however, much of the freight is otherwise taken care of, and the Trent Severn Waterway route is a popular sightseeing excursion, whether by houseboat, sailboat, cruiser or canoe.*

*The 384 kilometers (239 mi.) of gently meandering water passes through a dozen lakes, each as individual as its name suggests —Lovesick, Rice, Stony, Pigeon, Sparrow.*

*Only now you don't have to carry your boat, as Champlain did in several places nearly 400 years ago. A complete system of locks has been set up, their gates opening to let you through hamlets equally colorfully christened: Glen Ross, Rosedale, Gamebridge, Sawyer Creek, Nassau Mills...*

*One of the 44 locks has a hydraulic lift to accommodate the change in level of water. Another slides your craft up, or down, a marine railway chute.*

*Everything has been provided along the way—marinas, stores, accommodations and other facilities. You can fish for pike, maskinonge, pickerel (walleye) and bass, or you can swim, or simply sit back and enjoy the scenery.*

*Historic sites along the Trent Severn are marked. Among them is a monument to the Toronto area's first tourist, Samuel de Champlain, who had a much tougher time than you will navigating the route.*

# BLUEPRINT for a Perfect Trip

## How to Get There

Because of the complexity and variability of the many fares, you should ask the advice of an informed travel agent well before departure.

## BY AIR

### Scheduled flights

Toronto's international airport handles flights from practically all major U.S. cities and, of course, from all bigger Canadian towns, as well as from Central America, the Caribbean, Europe and the Middle East. Most flights from Australia and New Zealand connect through Los Angeles or Vancouver, while those from South Africa are routed via a European gateway city. Before booking the ticket, ask for any special excursion or winter/summer fares.

Average journey time from London is 8 hours, from New York, 1½ hours.

**Baggage:** Baggage allowances for scheduled transatlantic flights are complex, but you are allowed to check in, free, two suitcases of normal size. In addition, one piece of hand baggage of a size which fits easily under the aircraft seat may be carried on board. Check size and weight restrictions with your travel agent or air carrier when booking your ticket.

It is advisable to insure all luggage for the duration of your trip. Any travel agent can make the necessary arrangements.

### Charter flights and package tours

U.S. citizens can take advantage of a huge variety of charter flights and package tours. Remember to read your contract carefully.

Canada is a popular destination for British holiday-makers. While Toronto can be the sole destination, it is usually featured among other cities in a tour of Canada. Hotel accomodations and car rental may also be included.

From Australia, New Zealand and, to a lesser extent, South Africa, Toronto is visited as part of an overall tour of Canada and North America.

## BY RAIL

Coach rail fare can be very advantageous, especially at off-peak times. There is a train to Toronto daily from New York City and Chicago, while those traveling from the West Coast of the U.S. can connect with the *Transcontinental Canadian* at Vancouver. All trains arrive at Union Station, the southern point of Toronto's subway system.

## BY BUS

Even less expensive than the train, a good bus service is available from some major U.S. cities. *Greyhound/Trailways, Inc.* runs an express bus from New York City that covers the journey in 11 hours. Other buses leave Chicago and Detroit daily. From other U.S. cities, it is best to change in Buffalo or Montreal.

## BY CAR

Travelers from New York State, crossing the border at Buffalo, can take the Queen Elizabeth Way (QEW) to Toronto, which becomes the Gardiner Expressway leading downtown. Those crossing the border at Detroit should take Highway 401 (Macdonald-Cartier Freeway), taking one of the exits south to reach downtown. From the U.S. west, drive north and take the Trans-Canada Highway or, less scenic but probably faster, the interstate highways across the northern states.

# When to Go

Summer, June to August, is the best time to go, when the days are warm, with an average of eight to nine hours of sunshine. Winter can be severe, and the ground is usually snow-covered from mid-December to mid-March. Autumn and Spring can be very pleasant and colorful times of year.

The following chart gives average daily maximum temperatures in Toronto:

|      | J  | F  | M  | A  | M  | J  | J  | A  | S  | O  | N  | D  |
|------|----|----|----|----|----|----|----|----|----|----|----|----|
| °F   | 30 | 30 | 37 | 50 | 63 | 73 | 79 | 77 | 69 | 56 | 43 | 33 |
| °C   | -1 | -1 | 3  | 10 | 17 | 23 | 26 | 25 | 21 | 13 | 6  | 1  |

# Planning Your Budget

To give you an idea of what to expect, here's a sampling of average prices in Canadian dollars. They are approximate, as inflation is ever-present. Prices in Ottawa are generally lower than in Toronto.

**Airport transfer.** Gray Coach central subway lines: $5. Bus to main downtown hotels $9. Taxi to central Toronto about $30, plus tip.

**Car rental.** Weekend special with 200 km. free: $40 per day. Many weekend/weekly/monthly rental rates are available.

**Cigarettes.** $5.

**Entertainment.** Nightclub/discotheque $15 and up plus drinks; cinema $8; theater, concerts, ballet $15–125 (sometimes entry is free).

**Entrance fees.** Museums, adults $6; zoo, amusements parks, etc., $8. Children under 12, 30 to 50% less than regular prices. Senior citizens have reduced prices or free entry to many attractions, as do students with ID.

**Group tours.** Half to full-day tours of Toronto or Niagara Falls $65. $25 for half-day tour of Toronto.

**Hairdressers.** *Man's* haircut $15. *Woman's* cut from $15, shampoo and blow-dry $30, permanent wave or color rinse $45. Manicure $15.

**Hotels** $70 for lower-priced single room in one-star establishment to $200 double in five-star luxury hotel. Moderate double room $110.

**Meals and drinks.** Breakfast $7, snack bar or café lunch $10, restaurant meal $20, bottle of wine from $15, wine by the glass from $3.50, beer $3, cocktails from $5, soft drinks $1.50.

**Public transportation.** Subway, bus and streetcar one-way fare $1.25. Series of tickets and monthly pass available at lower rates.

**Taxis.** Drop rate $2.25, plus $0.50 per ⅕ mile.

# An A–Z Summary of Practical Information and Facts

**A**  **ACCOMMODATIONS.** (See also CAMPING.) The Ontario Ministry of Tourism publishes an extensive booklet listing several thousand places for tourists to stay, from top luxury hotels and resorts down to rooming houses, in all categories of size and price, located all over the province. Five stars is the top category, providing de-luxe accommodations, a complete gamut of shops, services, recreational facilities and so on. Four stars means excellent accommodations, high standards and extensive guest services. Three stars is still a high-quality hotel. Two stars means good accommodations and limited services. One star places offer adequate, clean lodging, with few guest services.

Size and type of lodging vary—from large hotels and motels to housekeeping resorts and fishing/hunting camps and lodges. In many towns, including Toronto and Stratford, bed and breakfast accommodations are offered by families.

For a free copy of the official government guide, *Accommodations,* write to Ontario Travel:

Queen's Park, Toronto, Ontario M7A 2R9

For detailed information and reservations, call Accommodation Toronto on (416) 369-9200; they will recommend varied accommodations at a price you can afford.

Another possibility is family-style farm vacations, listed in *Bed and Breakfast Associations and Farm Vacations;* many offer sports possibilities on or near the farm.

Try to reserve in advance, especially for summer vacations. Bookings can be very heavy in the peak season.

**Youth hostels.** Nine permanent hostels around the province offer reasonably priced accommodations. For details, contact Toronto International Hostel:

223 Church Street, Toronto, Ontario M5B 1Y7; tel. (416) 368-0207

or

Canadian Hostelling Association, National Office:

1600 James Naismith Dr., Suite 608, Gloucester, Ontario K1B 5N8; tel. (613) 748-5638

**AIRPORTS**. Toronto is served by Lester B. Pearson International (formerly Toronto International) Airport, 32 km. (20 miles) northwest of the city. Both national and international flights connect travelers with destinations all over America and on other continents. Toronto Island Airport, just opposite Harbourfront, is for small aircraft only.

Gray Coach Lines operates express buses between the airport and Islington, Yorkdale and York Mills subway stations every 40 minutes, from about 7 a.m. to midnight. Regular shuttle services also operate between several downtown hotels and motels and the airport: buses run every 20 minutes, the ride takes about 35 minutes.

Hamilton International Airport, located 68 km. (42 mi.) south of Toronto on the southwest tip of Lake Ontario, is convenient for visits to Toronto and southern Ontario. Niagara Falls is only 75 km. (47 mi.) southeast of the airport.

Ottawa is served by Ottawa International Airport, 18 km. (12 miles) south of town. A bus leaves about every 20 minutes for the major hotels. Full facilities are available at the airport. Rockcliffe Airport, a few miles northeast of town, serves smaller domestic airlines and is used by private aircraft.

On flights from Canada to the U.S. (international airports), passengers go through U.S. customs as they check in for their flight (and not after they have landed in the U.S.).

**BABY-SITTERS.** Most of the big downtown hotels and many motels in Toronto and Ottawa offer baby-sitting services (give the front desk as much advance notice as you can). Both cities also have several baby-sitting agencies (look in the *Yellow Pages* of telephone directories).

**BICYCLE RENTAL.** Both Toronto and Ottawa have well laid-out cycle paths, some of which pass through the city centers, so cycling can be a lot of fun. Ask your hotel desk or look in the *Yellow Pages* under "Bicycle Rentals".

The Canadian Hostelling Association (see ACCOMMODATIONS) organizes cycling tours through several interesting areas.

**CAMPING.** The Ontario Ministry of Tourism and Recreation puts out an excellent guide, *Camping,* which lists over 1,000 campsites by town, with complete information on location, nearest highway access and facilities.

**C**     Another booklet, *Outdoor Vacation Outfitters,* covers hiking trails, useful information on general travel, parks, permits and roads. To get free copies of these guides, write to Ontario Travel (see ACCOMMODATIONS).

Toronto's best campsite is the Glen Rouge Park at the city's eastern edge. It has nature trails and horse riding and is close to the huge Metro Zoo. There is also a campsite north of the city at Clairville Conservation Area near Downsview Airport.

**CAR RENTAL.** (See also DRIVING.) Cars may be rented at the international airports and in many cities and towns. Well-known international agencies and smaller firms offering ''budget'' prices have many types of car and RV (recreational vehicle) available. Agencies are listed in the *Yellow Pages* under ''Automobile Renting''.

For most companies, drivers must be 21 years or over, and hold a valid national license. The insurance rate is usually somewhat higher for drivers under 25. Major credit cards are generally accepted as payment.

**CIGARETTES, CIGARS, TOBACCO.** A few shops specialize in fine tobaccos, pipes and other paraphernalia. But cigarettes are usually sold in general shops, drugstores and hotel shops. Imported cigarettes tend to be slightly more expensive than locally made brands.

**CLIMATE and CLOTHING.** Though summer days tend to be hot and dry to muggy (especially around Toronto), you may hit a cool period —even in July—and in any case you should always have a jacket or sweater for the evening. A light raincoat and hat and/or umbrella are necessary, as well. In winter, be prepared for the cold with heavy wool or fur coats, warm sweaters, hats, gloves, boots or galoshes. People dress rather casually (especially the younger set who go for jeans and shorts in summer), but for business meetings and better restaurants you'll want more elegant wear.

## COMMUNICATIONS

**Post office hours** are generally 8 a.m. to 5:45 p.m., Monday through Friday. There are two post office locations with Saturday hours: Atrium on Bay, 595 Bay Street, 10 a.m. to 6 p.m. and First Canadian **112** Place, 100 King Street W., 10 a.m. to 5 p.m.

**Stamps** are sold at post offices, and at hotel desks, drugstores and other small shops with a Canada Post emblem on the window. Mailboxes are red and conveniently located on or near many street corners.

**General delivery (poste restante).** If you're expecting mail, and don't yet know your address, you can have it sent to general delivery at the main post office. Letters should carry a return address and be marked "Hold for 15 days" (the Canadian postal system will not hold mail longer). To collect mail, present suitable identification at the post office's General Delivery department.

**Telegrams.** This service is operated by CN/CP (Canadian National/ Canadian Pacific) Telecommunications—not the Post Office.

**Telephone.** The system is private, similar to that in the United States. Directions for payphones are posted inside booths. Long-distance and international calls can almost always be dialed direct from hotel rooms, but they're station-to-station calls. If you want person-to-person (personal) or a collect (reverse-charge) call, ask the operator to place it for you. Hotels usually add on an extra charge for calls. You can also charge calls on your U.S. telephone credit card.

The Toronto area code is 416, Ottawa 613. Dial 1 before the area code for long-distance calls (note that some calls within the 416 area are actually long-distance and you must dial 1 or 1-146 before the seven-digit number). Dial 0 (zero) for the operator and 411 for directory assistance (information).

**COMPLAINTS.** Managers or assistant managers of hotels and restaurants are nearly always available to assist you if you have complaints. The same applies to store owners and managers. Otherwise, contact the nearest Travel Information Centre or the Ontario Ministry of Tourism and Recreation for advice (see TOURIST INFORMATION OFFICES). Taxi companies will usually take up complaints about drivers, but you should know the driver's name and identification number (on display in the cab).

**CONSULATES and EMBASSIES**

In **Toronto**

**U.S.A.:**    Consulate-General, 360 University Avenue,
              Toronto M5G 1S4; tel. (416) 595-1700

**Great Britain:**    Consulate-General, Suite 1910, College Park,
                      777 Bay Street, Toronto M5G 2G2; tel. (416) 593-1290    **113**

**In Ottawa**

| | |
|---|---|
| **Australia:** | High Commission, 130 Slater St., Ottawa K1P 6L2; tel. (613) 236-0841 |
| **Eire:** | Embassy, 170 Metcalfe St., Ottawa K1P 1P3; tel. (613) 233-6281 |
| **Great Britain:** | High Commission, 80 Elgin Street, Ottawa K1P 5K7; tel. (613) 237-1530 |
| **New Zealand:** | High Commission, Suite 727, Metropolitan House, 99 Bank Street, Ottawa K1P 6G3; tel. (613) 238-5991 |
| **South Africa:** | Embassy, 15 Sussex Drive, Ottawa K1N 1M8; tel. (613) 744-0330 |
| **U.S.A.:** | Embassy, 100 Wellington Street, Ottawa K1P 5T1; tel. (613) 238-5335 |

**CONVERSION CHARTS.** (For fluid measures, see under DRIVING.) Canada uses the metric system for most measurements. You'll see road signs marked in kilometers, not miles. Weather reports are given in Celsius and Fahrenheit. Food and clothes may be measured by both the metric and American/British systems.

**Temperature**

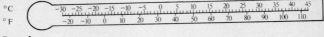

**Length**

**Weight**

**CRIME and THEFT.** While Toronto is still known for its miraculously low crime rate compared to other big cities, you're still advised to take the usual precautions. Be on the lookout for pickpockets in crowded concourses and the subway, lock your car and hotel room, and deposit valuables in the hotel safe.

**CUSTOMS CONTROLS and ENTRY FORMALITIES.** U.S. citizens must have some type of identification and proof of address (voter registration card, birth certificate or passport) to show the Canadian officials when entering and the U.S. authorities when returning. A driver's license is not accepted as identification. British subjects can no longer enter on a British Visitor's Passport. They, as well as citizens of most European and Commonwealth countries (including Australia and New Zealand) need a full passport—but no visa—to enter Canada. It's also necessary to have a return, or onward, ticket and enough money to cover your stay.

The following chart shows what main duty-free items you may take into Canada and, when returning home, into your own country:

| Into: | Cigarettes | Cigars | Tobacco | Liquor | Wine |
|---|---|---|---|---|---|
| Canada | 200 | and 50 | and 900 g. | 1.1 l. | or 1.1 l. |
| Australia | 200 | or 250 g. | or 250 g. | 1 l. | or 1 l. |
| Eire | 200 | or 50 | or 250 g. | 1 l. | and 2 l. |
| N.Zealand | 200 | or 50 | or 250 g. | 1.1 l. | and 4.5 l. |
| S. Africa | 400 | and 50 | and 250 g. | 1 l. | and 2 l. |
| U.K. | 200 | or 50 | or 250 g. | 1 l. | and 2 l. |
| U.S.A. | 200 | and 100 | and * | 1 l. | or 1 l. |

* a reasonable quantity

There's no limit to the amount of currency that can be imported or exported without declaration.

**DRIVING.** U.S. visitors taking their cars into Canada will need:

● a valid U.S. driver's license
● car registration papers
● a Canadian Non-Resident Interprovince Motor Vehicle Liability Insurance Card or evidence of sufficient insurance coverage to conform with local laws (available from your insurance agent)

Cars registered in the United States can be brought into Canada by the owner or his authorized driver for up to a year provided a form is filled out at the border. U.S. auto insurance is usually valid in 115

Canada; if in doubt, consult your agent. Note that if you rent a car in the U.S. to drive to Canada, at the border you'll have to show the rental contract, which must state that the car is intended for use in both Canada and the U.S.A.

European visitors taking their car to Canada will need:

- a valid driver's license
- car registration papers
- third-party insurance

For temporary importation of your car (up to six months), no special customs documents are necessary. But after that, you'll have to pass the Canadian driving test.

**Driving conditions.** Regulations are similar to those in the U.S.A. Drive on the right, pass on the left. Yield right of way to vehicles coming from your right at unmarked intersections. Roads are generally very good, with enough highway markers and directional signs to make finding your way easy. Toronto is well served with major arteries from every direction, including the famous QEW or Queen Elizabeth Way leading straight down to Niagara Falls and Buffalo. Maximum speed on expressways is 100 k.p.h. (60 m.p.h.); on regular country roads 80 k.p.h. (50 m.p.h.), and in school and central urban districts 40 k.p.h. (25 m.p.h.). The use of seat belts is obligatory and toddlers must be strapped into infant car seats. You may turn right on red lights if no traffic is coming through from the left, or unless otherwise indicated. When a school bus has stopped with red lights flashing, traffic in both directions must stop.

Driving conditions are usually quite relaxed, though caution should be observed. Things can get very crowded during rush hours in downtown Toronto, around the Gardiner Expressway and Queen's Quay fronting the harbor. Cars must stop at pedestrian crosswalks (marked by overhead signs and large painted Xs).

**Parking.** It is not usually a great problem, and many parking lots offer space for medium to high prices. But cars do get towed away for illegal parking, so beware. Never park in front of a fire hydrant. In Toronto, there is usually no parking or waiting on main streets during rush hours (7–9 a.m. and 4–6 p.m.).

**Breakdowns.** All over Toronto, Ottawa, Niagara Falls or wherever, you should have no problem in finding help if there's a mechanical difficulty. The expressways are patroled by the police and often have stopping-points where you can telephone for help if necessary. It is a good idea to belong to a big automobile organization such as the American Automobile Association or one of the two British equivalents—the AA and RAC—which are affiliated to the Canadian Automobile Association (CAA). Membership qualifies you for all sorts of insurance coverage, round-the-clock emergency breakdown assistance, tour planning, and so on. The CAA's head office is at:

2525 Carling Avenue, Ottawa, Ontario K1G 3T2;
tel. (613) 820-1890

Or you can contact the Toronto office:

2 Carlton Street, Toronto, Ontario M5B 1K4; tel. (416) 964-3111

**Gasoline (fuel) and oil.** There are plenty of filling stations throughout most of lower Ontario, but they are less commonly found up north around Thunder Bay, where you should take precautions and fill up before setting off into woodlands or relatively deserted lake areas. Gasoline comes in three types: regular, unleaded and premium or super unleaded. Diesel fuel is sold by the liter. Ontario has many self-service gas stations, or if you prefer to have an attendant fill the tank, check the oil and clean the windshield, choose the stations with service. Many stations also have clean eating and toilet facilities: truck stops on the highways generally offer the best food for the money and also keep the longest hours.

### Fluid measures

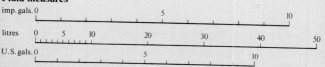

**Road signs.** In English, or self-evident international symbols. Speed limits are noted in kilometers.

**DRUGS.** It seems there were once some problems in various parts of Toronto, but if there are now, it certainly isn't obvious. Narcotics squads don't go around making frequent raids, but customs officials are very attentive, and if you're caught bringing in anything stronger than regular tobacco you might end up behind bars. In this health-minded part of the world, anything stronger than a few alcoholic drinks is *out*.

**E**  **ELECTRIC CURRENT.** The current is the same as in the U.S.—110–120-volt, 60-cycle AC. Plugs are the standard two-flat-prong American type, so Europeans should buy a plug adapter before they leave for Canada.

**EMERGENCIES.** Dial 911 for emergency calls to the police, fire department or ambulance service, all over Ontario.

Alternatively, dial 0 (zero) for the operator to get any kind of assistance.

**G**  **GUIDES and TOURS.** Information on day tours and private guides is available in hotels and through the Ontario Travel Centres (see TOURIST INFORMATION OFFICES).

**Toronto.** Apart from numerous guided bus tours, Toronto features inner city tours on a restored 1920s trolleycar and hourly boat tours around the harbor.

**Ottawa.** Student guides are available around Parliament Hill all year round, and bike around the center of town all summer to answer your questions and give advice. In summer, free downtown walking tours leave every 15 minutes from the Visitor Centre, Elgin and Sparks streets.

**Niagara Falls.** Guided tours on foot (raincoats and boots provided) or by limousine, double-decker bus, boat or helicopter.

**Hamilton.** City bus tours leave from downtown, where the major shopping area can be found. As the most recently developed entry point for southern Ontario, Hamilton has several sightseeing points of note, including the Canadian Football Hall of Fame, Art Gallery and 1,012-hectare (2,500-acre) Royal Botanical Gardens.

**H**  **HEALTH and MEDICAL CARE.** (See also EMERGENCIES.) Large hotels have a nurse and doctor on call at all times. Hospital care is of a very high standard, and emergency rooms generally give swift and efficient service. But medical fees can be costly, so make sure your health insurance will cover you while in Canada. Visitors may also obtain health insurance coverage from the Ontario Blue Cross, a non-profit organization affiliated with the one in the U.S. Details of the

plans and application forms may be obtained directly from Ontario
Blue Cross:

150 Ferrand Drive, Don Mills, Ontario M3C 1H6; tel. (416) 429-2661

People with special problems (diabetes, epilepsy, heart condition) can
subscribe, for a small fee, to various services which issue laminated
cards stating your condition, in case of emergencies, and keep a file of
medical history available at all times.

Besides the annoyance of blackflies and mosquitoes (and they can
be really pesky up in the woodlands and around lakes), there are no
special health problems in Ontario. Summer heat and winter cold
might be exhausting to anybody used to less extreme climates. If
you're going into the summer sun, take the usual sun-screen precautions; the sun can burn you on a lake as fiercely as it might in the
Aegean Sea.

**Pharmacies**, or drugstores, are generally open 7 a.m. to 10 or 10:30
p.m., Monday through Friday. If you need something after-hours or
on weekends, inquire at your hotel desk.

**HITCHHIKING.** As in the United States, it's out of favor nowadays,
except perhaps with hikers up north and in the vast park areas; even
here, the climate of mistrust has set it. Thumbing is illegal on the
expressways, though it is permitted on the approach roads.

**LANGUAGE.** English is the language you'll hear most all over Ontario, except for Ottawa, which is almost bilingual, with French-speaking Hull just across the river in Quebec. But of course among the
throngs of immigrants in the various Toronto neighborhoods, you're
likely to hear Italian, German, Chinese, maybe even Urdu. Americanisms have definitely crept into this once very Scots and British part
of the world, although in many cases British rather than American
terms are still used.

**LAUNDRY and DRY-CLEANING.** All the better hotels will arrange
to have laundry and dry-cleaning done on weekdays, often with same-day service for an additional price. There are a few hand laundries
in Toronto's Chinatown (Dundas Street), and coin-operated laundromats throughout Toronto and Ottawa.

**L**  **LEGAL HOLIDAYS.** When a holiday falls on a Sunday, the next day is often observed as the holiday. There are eight official holidays, when all government offices and most businesses are closed:

| | |
|---|---|
| New Year's Day | January 1 |
| Good Friday | |
| Victoria Day | Monday before May 25 |
| Canada Day | July 1 |
| Labor Day | 1st Monday in September |
| Thanksgiving Day | 2nd Monday in October |
| Christmas Day | December 25 |
| Boxing Day | December 26 |

**LIQUOR LAWS.** The only way to buy liquor (spirits) and imported wines is in LCBOs (shops run by the Liquor Control Board of Ontario), of which there are several in every city, usually open 10 a.m. to 6 p.m., Monday through Saturday. Some LCBOs are open later: check the *Yellow Pages* for addresses. Minimum drinking age is 19. Drinking hours in licensed establishments are 11 a.m. to 1 a.m., Monday through Saturday, noon to 1 a.m., Sunday. It is against the law to carry around an open can of beer or an opened bottle of wine or liquor.

**LOST AND FOUND.** The Toronto Transit Commission's Lost Articles is at the Bay Street Subway Station, tel. (416) 393-4100, open 8 a.m. to 5:30 p.m., Monday through Friday.

If your children stray in one of those delightful theme and amusement parks, guides and information services can help you find them easily. People in stores and museums are also very helpful.

**M**  **MAPS.** Good maps of Ontario and some city maps are available from the Ministry of Tourism (see TOURIST INFORMATION OFFICES).

The maps in this guide were prepared by Falk-Verlag, Hamburg.

**MEETING PEOPLE.** There's no reason to feel lonely in Ontario, since most people are open, friendly and smiling. If you don't already have business or personal contacts (who will introduce you to *their* friends), you can meet people just about anywhere from shops and parks to bars and restaurants. You might make new acquaintances in a movie line or at a sidewalk café, or ice-skating, or shuffling along on cross-country skis. Everybody converses casually in any situation. Women (and of course men) can go alone just about anywhere.

You can arrange a whole vacation around meeting Canadian families; the Ontario Ministry of Tourism's brochure *Bed and Breakfast Associations and Farm Vacations* lists farm vacations—some with tennis and swimming facilities on or near the premises; and in towns like Stratford you can stay with local families in attractive homes, approved by committees promoting tourism.

## MONEY MATTERS

**Currency.** Both official languages, English and French, appear on the Canadian dollar; all bills are the same size, but the several denominations are of different colors.

Coins: 1, 5, 10, 25 and 50 cents and 1 dollar.

Bills: 1, 2, 5, 10, 20, 50, 100, 500 and 1,000 dollars.

The Canadian coin names are the same as the American: penny, nickel, dime, quarter, half-dollar and one-dollar.

**Banks and currency-exchange offices.** Standard banking hours are 10 a.m. to 3 p.m. Monday through Thursday; 10 a.m. to 6 p.m. Friday. Most trust companies are open 9 a.m. to 5 p.m. weekdays and on Saturday mornings. Many banks have branches with extended evening and Saturday hours as well as bank machines for customer convenience. The best exchange rate, no matter what the currency, is at banks, although some major hotels will exchange U.S. currency and traveler's checks.

When changing money or traveler's checks, ask for 1- to 20-dollar bills, which are accepted everywhere, as some establishments do not take larger banknotes. For transactions of this sort, take your passport, for identification.

**Credit cards and traveler's checks.** The major credit cards and well-known traveler's checks in Candian—*not U.S.*—dollars are accepted throughout Canada at banks, hotels, restaurants, most shops and many filling stations. Carry some official identification.

## NEWSPAPERS and MAGAZINES. 
Worldwide news coverage is excellent, and Toronto itself has three thriving dailies, *The Globe and Mail, The Sun* and *The Toronto Star*. At most newsstands, many in

hotels, you can purchase a wide variety of dailies and weekly magazines from New York, London, Paris and other parts of the world. In better hotels, room service delivers the paper of your choice along with breakfast.

**PETS**. Cats and dogs entering from the United States must be accompanied by a certificate signed by a vet declaring that the animal has been vaccinated against rabies within the preceding 36 months. Pets from other countries may be subject to special regulations, so it's best to check with a Canadian consulate or information service before you leave home. On return to Great Britain or Eire, a dog will have to be kept in quarantine for six months; the United States reserves the right to quarantine returning animals as well.

Some large hotels allow animals, and may even have special kennels, but it's best to check on their rules in advance.

**PHOTOGRAPHY**. All kinds of film, cameras and photographic equipment are readily available in towns and cities, although sometimes slightly more expensive than in the United States. Inquire about camera discount houses, such as those around Yonge Street in Toronto. Camera shops usually give the fastest development service, though you can sometimes find 24-hour processing in drugstores as well.

**POLICE.** (See also EMERGENCIES.) Of all police forces, the federal RCMP (Royal Canadian Mounted Police, or "Mounties") are the most colorful in their red coats and big hats. You'll see them frequently in Ottawa, but hardly anywhere else, in their scarlet ceremonial uniforms. The RCMP provide the federal policing as well as the provincial and territorial policing, by contract, in all of Canada except the provinces of Quebec and Ontario. Around Ontario, you will see the Ontario Provincial Police, wearing blue uniforms, patroling in black-and-white cars. Toronto's force is the Metropolitan Toronto Police, wearing blue, usually driving white cars.

**RADIO and TELEVISION.** CBC (Canadian Broadcasting Corporation) is the biggest broadcaster in both media, but it by no means has a monopoly. Most hotels have television in the room, and you can enjoy a variety of stations and networks from both the United States and Canada. Both Ottawa and Toronto have radio FM-stereo networks specializing in classical or jazz programs.

**RELIGIOUS SERVICES.** Almost every type of religion and religious sect is represented in Toronto. Protestants and Roman Catholics hold a clear majority, but there are also mosques, synagogues and Hindu and Buddhist temples. Your hotel desk and the weekend newspapers can help you find out addresses and times of services.

**TIME DIFFERENCES.** Most of Ontario, including Toronto, Ottawa and Niagara Falls, is on Eastern Time, the same as New York and the entire U.S. east coast. Regions west of 90° longitude, around Thunder Bay, are on Central Time, one hour earlier. From the last Sunday in April until the last Saturday in October, clocks are advanced one hour for Daylight Saving Time.

| Los Angeles | Chicago | **Toronto** | Halifax | London | Paris |
|-------------|---------|-------------|---------|--------|-------|
| 9. a.m. | 11 a.m. | **noon** | 1 p.m. | 5 p.m. | 6 p.m. |

**TIPPING.** As in the United States, a service charge is not normally included in hotel and restaurant bills, so tipping is customary. You may use your discretion for good or poor service, but here are some guidelines:

| | |
|---|---|
| Hotel porter, per bag | 75¢ |
| Maid, per day | $1–2 |
| Waiter | 15% |
| Hairdresser/Barber | 10–15% |
| Taxi driver | 10–15% |
| Tour guide | 10% |

**TOILETS.** Ontarians will probably understand you if you ask for the "rest-room", "washroom", "lavatory", "loo" or "john". Nowa- **123**

T days these conveniences are usually marked with pictographs for men or women. They are mostly clean and easily found in filling stations, museums, subway stops, cafés or bars (where they'd rather you buy a drink), as well as the shopping complexes, above or below ground. If there are attendants, you should leave a tip.

**TOURIST INFORMATION OFFICES.** The Ontario Ministry of Tourism and the Canadian Government Office of Tourism operate information services in many countries. These will supply you with a host of brochures and maps covering everything from hotels and transportation to special vacations and accommodations.

Canadian Government offices abroad:

**Australia:** 8th floor, AMP Centre, 50 Bridge Street, Sydney 2000; tel. (02) 231-6522

**Great Britain:** Macdonald House, 1 Grosvenor Square, London W1X 0AB; tel. (071) 629-9492

**U.S.A.:** Offices in most major cities.

For information on **Canada:**

Tourism Canada, 235 Queen Street, Ottawa, Ontario K1A 0H5; tel. (613) 954-3980

For information on **Ontario:**

Ontario Travel, Queen's Park, Toronto, Ontario M7A 2E5; tel. (416) 965-4008 Monday through Friday 8 a.m. to 6 p.m. (extended hours in summer). Toll-free from U.S.A. 1-800-ONTARIO (668-2746). They also have an office in the Eaton Centre, 290 Yonge Street, Eaton's, 2 Below, Monday to Friday, 10 a.m. to 9 p.m., Saturday, 9:30 a.m. to 6 p.m.

Tourist Information in **Toronto** and **Ottawa:**

Metropolitan Toronto Convention and Visitors' Association, Queen's Quay Terminal at Harbourfront, P.O. Box 126, 207 Queen's Quay West, Toronto, Ontario M5J 1A7; tel. (416) 368-9821 Monday through Friday 8:30 a.m. to 5 p.m., Saturdays and Sundays 10 a.m. to 5 p.m.

An information booth is open year-round outside the Eaton Centre and SkyDome and, during the summer, there are other booths around the city at Nathan Phillips Square, the Royal Ontario Museum, Convention Centre, Harbourfront, and Mel Lastman Square, North York.

Canada's Capital Visitor and Convention Bureau, Visitor Information Centre, National Arts Centre, 65 Elgin Street at Confederation Square, Ottawa K1P 5W1; tel. (613) 237-5158 7 days, daytime only.

National Capital Commission Centre, 10 Metcalfe Street, Ottawa K1K 6J6; tel. (613) 239-5000 7 days, daytime only.

City of Ottawa Information Centre, Frelman Mall, 73 Rideau Street, Ottawa K1N 5W8; tel. (613) 564-1415 Monday through Saturday.

## TRANSPORTATION

**Toronto.** The Toronto Transit Commission (TTC) assures easy travel around town even if you aren't driving yourself. The efficient, safe and clean **subway** (underground) is renowned; it covers the city in a north-south loop, plus lines east and west. Hours: Monday to Saturday 6 a.m.–1:30 a.m. and Sunday 9 a.m.–1:30 a.m. Tel. (416) 393-4636.

**Buses and streetcars** cover the city quite thoroughly. You can get a free transfer if you need both subway and bus or streetcar one way from A to B. Buses accept only exact fare or ticket-transfer bought in subway stations. The King Street streetcar and some buses run 24 hours a day.

**Ottawa.** Bus routes are operated by the Ottawa-Carleton Regional Transit Commission (OC TRANSPO), offering maps in their main office at 294 Albert Street. If you don't have the required one-way exact fare, you can buy tickets at some tabacco and other shops.

**Taxis** are readily available at taxi stands, especially near hotels, important concourses, railroad stations, and so on. They can also be hailed in the street or phoned from your hotel or elsewhere.

**Trains.** GO (Government of Ontario) Transit services connect Toronto's Union Station with the outer suburbs, as far as Hamilton; tel. (416) 630-3933. Buses also, outside town.

VIA Rail operates all over Canada. The Toronto terminal is Union Station at Bay and Front streets: tel. (416) 366-8411. The Ottawa terminal is on St. Laurent Boulevard, a good way southeast of the city center: tel. (613) 238-8289.

**WATER.** Tap water is safe to drink. Most hotels and motels provide an ice machine in the corridor or stairwell, often alongside a soft-drink dispenser. Well-known brands of Canadian and French mineral water can be purchased in shops and markets, as well as better restaurants.

# Index

An asterisk (*) next to page number indicates a map reference. Where there is more than one set of page references, the one in bold type refers to the main entry. For index to Practical Information, see inside front cover.

INDEX

049/102 SUD18